The Wisdom Within

Cracking the Secrets of Meaning, Purpose, & Security

Lara Jaye

Copyright

The Wisdom Within: Cracking the Secrets of Meaning, Purpose, & Security

Copyright © 2023 Lara Habig and Lara Jaye LLC

Published by Lara Habig and Lara Jaye

Cover Design: Rachel Dunham, Brand Therapy

Editor: Christine Haden

Layout & Design: Clark Kenyon

All rights reserved. No part of this book may be used or reproduced in any form without the written permission from the copyright owners. Without prior permission, it is theft of the author's intellectual property. Brief quotations embodied in articles and reviews without prior written permission of the publisher is permissible. Thank you in advance!

For general information or to get in the touch with the author visit: LaraJaye.com.

Disclaimer: Although every effort to ensure that the information in this book was correct at press time, neither assume and hereby disclaim any liability to any party for any loss, damage, or disruption caused by errors or omissions, whether such errors or omissions result from negligence, accident, or any other cause. Names have been changed to protect the privacy of some parties.

ISBN: 978-0-9984728-1-2 (Hardcover)
       978-0-9984728-2-9 (Paperback)
       978-0-9984728-4-3 (eBook)
       978-0-9984728-3-6 (Audiobook)

Printed in the United States of America.

Dedication

Dedicated to my sons, Daniel and Tyler, and my sister, Lisa, who may not always agree with or understand me yet lovingly support me anyway.

And, to all the souls who desire to know themselves at a deeper level, this book is for YOU!

Raving Reviews

"Lara's deeply moving narrative weaves a heartfelt tale that serves as a guiding star in the midst of emotional chaos and the depths of soul-searching, showing the way toward healing and wholeness. In a world where every individual grapples with their unique emotional challenges, **Lara's insights pave the way for a profound inward exploration that connects us to the Source of our being.** Through expertly designed guided meditations and contemplative exercises, Lara reveals how even the most entrenched emotional scars can shift into a transformative journey, becoming a precious facet of human growth and the human experience."

~**Jean Slatter, Author of *Hiring the Heavens*, Creative Mystic**

"This will become one of my favorite, well-worn reference books with lots of underlining, highlighting and personal notes tucked in it. Once again, **Lara has captured the essence of our fragile human conditions** and put words to the accompanying ugly layers of darkness that plague us. Be prepared to confront it - that which knows no boundary of age, time or our supposed economic and social status - and be guided into the healing, loving LIGHT."

~**Jennie Boller**

"Many thanks to Lara for having the courage to bare her soul to write *The Wisdom Within*, a **revelatory handbook for energy healing**, full of pearls and relatable stories using memorable visualizations to help us learn. *The Wisdom Within* is a welcome and much-needed additional tool in my spiritual toolchest."

~**Joan Koewler Suleskey**

"As a physician trained in typical Western medicine in women's health, I frequently encounter patients grappling with the same issues highlighted in *The Wisdom Within*. The availability of **numerous unconventional, 'out-of-the-box' healing options is truly remarkable**. If individuals were to invest their energy and commitment into actively addressing their issues rather than seeking quick fixes, the potential for improved and longer lasting results would be substantial. So many of us need education and guidance on using these methods that are new to most of us, although ancient to those who have been enlightened. Thank you Lara for giving us the basic information and homework to get us going!"

~Barbara A. Koewler, JD, FACOG

"Absolutely amazing how everything is explained through story and experience with definitions, guidance, and tools on how to energetically navigate every aspect of our lives. This book is a genius in flow allowing for an easy read you don't want to put down. **A bible for our radical, awakening time!**"

~Amanda Masters, Awake Universe

"I have known Lara since she was a little girl in a small town. In this book, Lara bears her soul. I learned so much about what she does and how she is helping us all. Many things she has done that have made people scratch their heads and question her are explained, but that is not its purpose. *The Wisdom Within* will help you connect to your inner self. If we need more help than the book, she has literally lived it. She provides meditations and explanations to help you get there. Others may be experiencing some of what Lara experiences and don't understand what is happening. She can help the novice understand what their purpose is. How we react to the world or how we shield ourselves from the world is what affects our happiness and peacefulness. She **helps her readers acknowledge, interpret, and**

open themselves up as they become more in tune with energy around them. Lucky are those who meet Lara. She is an inspiration!"

~**Glenda Meyer**

"Lara is a dear friend and trusted spiritual healer. I was very excited to read this book. It did not disappoint! It is **a roadmap to spiritual awakening, spiritual care, and spiritual guidance**. It is also a great book to keep on hand for reference as circumstances arise that need our attention. BRAVO, Lara!"

~**Janet Zildjian, RN**

"Lara has done it again, yet this time, with even more openness. This book is a MUST-READ for anyone who thinks the awakening process is easy. It's the real and sometimes ugly integration process of a woman who is determined to help shine more light and love on the planet in whatever way she can."

~**Beth Shaw**

"*The Wisdom Within: Cracking the Secrets of Meaning, Purpose, & Security* will help millions of souls on planet earth who are awakening to their power yet still dredging through sludge in their life. Lara Jaye's **work is pure, authentic, and honest**. You don't want to miss this book!"

~**Amber A.**

"Without being preachy or judgy, Lara Jaye's newest book walks us through several dark nights to give us tips and tools for success in our own lives. Her natural honesty demonstrates a woman who **walks her talk in her own imperfect way**."

~**Sierra A.**

"For a woman who didn't want to write this book, Lara has hit a home run out of the ballpark! Her willingness to dive deep into the root of her pain with her unique intuitive tools and tips for healing **is** an example to all of us not to be afraid of what lurks underneath. Light and love can overcome anything!"

~Jenna B.

"**Dark, stormy, yet full of light and love.** Every page leaps out at you, helping you recognize where there are unhealed parts of yourself while giving you tools and tips to heal yourself!"

~Zac M.

"God-lead, Spirit infused, Lara Jaye's newest book, *The Wisdom Within*, is a journey of an incredibly intuitive and sensitive woman who continues to get knocked down and back up again. Although wounded in the battle, her resilience shines brightly as she intuitively makes her way through each day."

~Amala

"There isn't much this woman hasn't experienced. Lara Jaye's authentic and organic spirit draws the reader near as they connect with some part of something she's been through. She tells her honest story and thoroughly walks you through her own process of meeting her demons and what she did when she met them. **This is a MUST-READ for anyone ready to dive deep into themselves with love and support.**"

~Patricia P.

"**Mesmerizing** — Lara will have you on the edge of your seat reading her true story of leading a courageous life often ridiculed by outside observers."

~Lucas L.

Contents

	Introduction	1
1	Walking Alone	23
2	Family Traditions	35
3	She Talks to Angels	51
4	Words are Energy	68
5	Mind Games	81
6	Learning to Fly	96
7	Time to Move On	108
8	Our House	121
9	Dancing With Your Shadows	138
10	Just Be Held	153
11	Jumping Timelines	171
12	Sweet Emotions	186
13	Lonely People	205
14	Everything is Energy	217
15	Unwritten	234
	What's Next?	243
	About the Author	244
	References	245

Dear Reader

Thank you for following your guidance to open *The Wisdom Within: Cracking the Secrets of Meaning, Purpose, & Security*.

While praying about the concept of this creation, I found myself hesitant to write this particular story. I knew it needed to be told, yet, instead, I asked God, "Can't I write something else? Perhaps something lighter, more cheery?" I intuitively heard back, "You have already written that. It's time for this."

My reaction? Well, let's just say it wasn't the most enthusiastic. Yes, my response to the Divine, the Almighty Spirit, presenting me with the conception of a book was, well, rather dismissive.

And the reason why is that I knew what was ahead. As I engage in the act of writing, I find myself immersed in the very fabric of the narrative. This was not designed to be a lighthearted and breezy composition. Our trajectory was aimed at the profound depths, and there we went indeed. God knew exactly what I needed, guiding me through the complicated passages of this journey.

As you embark on your own quest within, several approaches exist to engage with its content. The story unfolds beginning with the introduction as a foundation. If you find yourself guided, you can read the book linearly, immersing yourself in its entirety before revisiting each chapter introspectively to journal and extract the profound insights that can only emerge from a contemplative inward exploration. Alternatively, you might decide to savor the experience, progressing deliberately—one chapter per week, capturing the precious gems that rise to the surface as you go along.

Regardless of your chosen path, I encourage you to relish the unique Light Language Meditations thoughtfully composed for each chapter. By using your smartphone, access your photo application and direct your device to hover over the QR code located at the end of each chapter. This action will prompt a web address to materialize. Click on this link, and it will seamlessly transport you to an exclusive webpage, thoughtfully curated for YOU, thus enhancing your encounter with its essence. I highly recommend you visit LaraJaye.com often to be the first to know about the upcoming virtual class that pairs with the book, as well.

Within your hands, you do not merely hold a compilation of written words; you possess a dynamic instrument of healing potential. Much like all of my creations, I have infused *The Wisdom Within: Cracking the Secrets of Meaning, Purpose, & Security* with light language healing codes. I invite you to welcome the healing energy of unadulterated Divine Love that emanates from the text, infusing your heart, body and soul as you absorb its pages.

It is with a deep sense of reverence that I am honored to be on this journey with you. Much love and blessings on your adventure into yourself.

Lara

Introduction

Weary traveler
Beat down from the storms that you have weathered
Feels like this road just might go on forever
Carry on You keep on givin'

But every day this world just keeps on takin'
Your tired heart is on the edge of breaking
Carry on

~Jordan St. Cyr

In the Spring of 2017, my mom transitioned to the Heavenly realms, and a couple of months later, unexpectedly and unrelated, two of my young nephews passed away within ten days of each other. I was also traveling internationally and had an emergency surgery. My days began to blur while my heart was heavy with grief. As I flew to Indiana from Florida on a Friday night for the third family funeral in two months, my dad greeted me aghast, curious why I wasn't home working. I will never forget the look on his face—furious that I had spent the money to return for another funeral and, worse yet, that I wasn't doing something at that moment to make more money. Instead, I was spending it on seemingly frivolous traveling.

Coming from a long line of entrepreneurs, I learned the value of working hard very early. Although my inner motto was always *people before things*, the messages infused in me were quite the opposite. I suspect it was also a common generational imprint of my dad's era to hold the fear of money regardless of the reason behind spending it.

There I stood, frozen, disagreeing with my dad about spending money to travel to a family funeral, and I wasn't going to win this argument. I grabbed my suitcase, checked into a nearby hotel in my hometown, and cried myself to sleep. I returned to Florida a few days later, feeling even more sad that I had disappointed my dad.

I was growing weary. It's a familiar feeling that many people experience at various points in their lives. It can be caused by physical or mental exhaustion, stress, or a lack of motivation. When you're weary, finding the energy and motivation to do anything can be challenging, which can cause a vicious circle of frustration and overwhelm. Feelings of apathy, lack of motivation, and hopelessness can accompany it. It's not uncommon to feel weary after a long period of stress or overworking, but it can also be a symptom of depression or other mental health issues.

Weariness means exhaustion at the core. You may feel battered over and over, like a wave continuing to crash into you as you try to swim back to shore. Instead, it seems you are getting further and further off course. Not only are you further away from the coast, but seemingly off on a whole other trajectory. You pray fervently that each batter of the wave doesn't pull you down by the undertow. Relentless waves of energy, chaos, toxic people, events, natural disasters, job loss, and health issues continue to suck us under, causing us to question our very existence.

Unfortunately, weariness is a term I have often used over the last couple of decades. Sometimes I even felt like I'd been dragged down a gravel road. Weariness overwhelmed me when I was physically ill and depressed while going through a divorce after twenty-five years of marriage. Like putting a coat on, I would put on my familiar weariness energy while dragging myself through the day.

Even in my weariness, I am reminded that all is being used for the

Introduction

greater good and nothing is ever wasted. Regardless, the next few years after the divorce weren't much of a reprieve. I was struggling to find my place in the world. Basics like where to live, how to earn income, and making friends were at the top of my daily worry list. My weariness continued.

Life is busy, and generally, there is little time to go within. We have places to go—traffic to maneuver. People to see. Family dinners and children's lunches to prepare. Deadlines to meet. Meetings to attend. Phone calls and emails to return. As 2020 began, what was ahead of us was just more of the same. That is, until the world shut down.

The pandemic hit hard and fast. Siesta Key, Florida—the #1 Beach in America (where I lived then) was closed—even during their busy season. Streets were empty of bustling people, while the live music and loud cars were silenced. With a compromised immune system, toilet paper shortages, and a closed business where I saw clients, life quickly came to a screeching halt. I took a few days to catch my breath while plotting my next pivot. Connecting to myself became my guiding light. Within my own silence, I began to see that I could create any life I chose. During this time, I also tapped into the infinite source of creation to begin allowing it to unfold in divine timing.

We all have stories of where we were and who we were with in lockdown as we were pushed to edges we didn't even know we had. Whether it was six weeks like for me in Florida or years in other countries, we all grew tired very quickly of the same four walls. Medical professionals were working themselves to the bone while others were sent home—most not even paid. Many industries—restaurants, fitness trainers, and others were forced to create a new way forward. Others chose to close their doors for good. Our world hasn't been the same since, nor will it ever be. We are living in an incredibly unique time in history, and these unprecedented times invite us to dive deep into our psyche.

Doing this inner work for the last couple of decades, I thought I knew exactly who I was and what I wanted. I wanted to be living my life in a divine, surrendered flow. I wanted to be at the perfect place at the perfect time. I wanted divine synchronicity to run my days. But most of all, I wanted chaos in my life to be eliminated, deeper relationships, balance, and harmony to be restored to my hours, and I specifically wanted to expand my healing and intuitive abilities.

During my lockdown time on Siesta, I would meander to the couch with my coffee in hand, stillness calling my name, and the wind dancing above the ocean waves. Gratitude, meditation, prayers, and more would pour through my head and heart. I would address the endless mind chatter to hear the still, small voice within. In this stillness, moments seemed to freeze yet pass quickly. This was my time to regroup and just BE. I was ever thankful for the slowdown of the world. It seemed like a welcome time-out from the Universe. It afforded almost all of us an extended time to rethink if we were living our best lives. I would ask myself while journaling, "Am I living out the highest expression of myself? What even is my highest expression?" Without embracing stillness in our everyday lives, we stumble through the noise and take guesses at our next pivot. We cannot honor ourselves and our true calling when we have no idea what it is. Only in the quiet can we hear our soul whispering to us.

The road would take me deeper within to achieve the path I so desperately desired, especially to those dark places inside that I had intentionally ignored. You know the place where we want to numb ourselves and not feel. Yes—that's the spot! That's the sweet spot of stuck trauma that needs attention. Layer by layer, I would uncover another nugget of something that needed my love. I focused on my mind, body, emotions, Spirit, and energy field. The unseen energy that is barely, if at all, visible to the human eye. To achieve that deep connection with myself I craved, I took each area one by one, day by day, while

Introduction

staying focused on the life I wanted to create. By doing this, I was soon catapulted to a firm foundation of self-trust, self-love, and resilience I never thought possible.

Every living soul on our planet is experiencing this metamorphosis at some level. As Earth's frequency is being upgraded, we are simultaneously being triggered to examine ourselves at a deeper level. We are all invited to move through this shift of consciousness with more self-awareness. To do this, we observe our behavior, heal our trauma, and embrace self-responsibility.

We are shifting from...

> Struggle to FLOW
> Doing to BEING
> Stress to PEACE
> Confusion to CLARITY
> Chaos to POWER and
> Competition to COOPERATION AND CONNECTION

I believe many of us thought that this process of awakening, raising our frequency, and moving through this SHIFT—personally and collectively—would be more rainbows and lollipops. Creating that higher vibe life by co-creating with Spirit will take some tearing apart of the old structures. Your life in the rearview mirror that you held onto so tightly needs time to collapse while building a new stronger foundation. Those old beliefs and patterns that supported us must go. It may even be gut-wrenching and challenging to give up some pieces you held dearly. If you don't know this already, you will by the end of this book:

The way OUT of chaos is IN.

The way OUT of disconnection is IN.

The way OUT of numbing yourself is IN.

To thine own self be true. This is the way to a life of flow, balance, and harmony. To be true to ourselves, we must meet the self we have ignored. You know that self, the one you shoved down when it wanted to tell you something. The self that was screaming for attention so it sparked pain in your body. The self you don't want to look at in the mirror.

Is something stirring inside of you?

Does your soul want your attention?

It's a strange feeling that can be difficult to put into words, yet it's something that many people experience at some point in their lives. It is a calling to slow down to get quiet while getting honest with yourself. First, we must NOTICE and BE AWARE that our soul asks for our observation.

While the concept of the soul varies depending on your beliefs and culture, it generally refers to the essence of you. Your soul is the part of you that exists beyond your physical body and your thoughts, emotions, and beliefs. It's often described as the source of your inner wisdom and intuition and connected to the greater Universe or divine energy. When your soul tries to get your attention, you might experience a range of sensations and emotions. Common signs are restlessness, heightened intuition, vivid dreams, meaningful coincidences or synchronicities, and physical sensations.

This introductory chapter provides a "Readers Digest" version of what is happening collectively and how it may affect us each personally.

Introduction

Understanding the cycle our planet is currently experiencing is imperative in digesting Spirit's higher purposes. This chapter outlines the processes and explains various terms I use throughout the book for a better understanding.

Our Planet's Metamorphism

Our planet's evolutionary metamorphism is a fascinating topic that has captured the attention of scientists and spiritual leaders alike. According to recent research, we are experiencing the end of a 26,000-year-old cycle, causing significant changes in our planet's evolutionary journey.

This cycle is known as the precession of the equinoxes. It is a slow, gradual movement of the Earth's axis that causes the position of the stars to shift over time. The precession of the equinoxes is divided into twelve equal parts, each lasting approximately 2,160 years, and is associated with a particular astrological sign.

We are transitioning from the Age of Pisces to the Age of Aquarius, which marks the end of this 26,000-year-old cycle. As a significant transition period for our planet, we can expect to see changes in our political, economic, social systems, as well as changes in our environment and climate. Many believe the focus on materialism, greed, and individualism that characterized the Age of Pisces will turn to a focus on spirituality, unity, and community which will mark the Age of Aquarius. As we move into the Age of Aquarius, there is a growing awareness of the impact of human activity on the planet and a greater emphasis on sustainability and environmental stewardship.

Navigating this transition period requires us to cultivate a sense of openness, adaptability, and resilience. Cultivating mindfulness, staying informed, and embracing change are all necessary in transition. We are invited to be open to new ideas, perspectives, and ways of doing things. While this transition may be challenging, it also presents an opportunity for growth and positive change. We can navigate this transition period successfully and contribute to a more sustainable and harmonious future for our planet. As with any ending and new beginnings, there are transitions and overlaps to make it as smooth as possible. This transformation is ushering us all into a cycle of ascension.

Ascension

Ascension is a term that is often used in spiritual circles to describe a process of personal and collective transformation that is taking place on the planet. It refers to an elevation in consciousness as we move towards a higher spiritual awareness and understanding level. At its core, ascension is about becoming more fully aligned with our highest selves and the Universe's divine energies. It involves shedding old beliefs and patterns of behavior that no longer serve us and opening ourselves up to new levels of wisdom and understanding.

Here are some key ways ascension affects us individually—

1. **Increased awareness:** As we ascend, we become more aware of our thoughts, feelings, and actions. We begin to recognize patterns in our behavior that may hold us back, and we start seeing the world around us with new eyes.
2. **Expanded consciousness:** Ascension involves an expansion of our consciousness beyond the limits of our physical bodies and the material world. We begin to recognize that there is more to life than what we can see and touch, and we explore the Universe's more profound mysteries.
3. **Healing and transformation:** As we become more aligned with our highest selves, we may experience profound healing and transformation in all areas of our lives. We may find that old wounds and traumas are healed and that we can move forward with greater clarity, purpose, and joy.
4. **Connection with others:** As we ascend, we may feel more

connected to others on a deeper level. We may feel a sense of unity and interconnectedness with all beings and find that we can connect with others more authentically and meaningfully.

While the ascension process may be complex, it ultimately allows us to live a more fulfilling and purposeful life. By opening ourselves up to new levels of awareness, consciousness, and understanding, we can experience profound transformation and growth and become more fully aligned with our highest selves and the divine energies of the Universe.

We are living in uncertain and chaotic times. Regardless of what we call it, we all can agree something massive is going on, which is a quickening of time. Bumps and bruises along the way are expected while we are transitioning.

The terms "lightworker" and "light warrior" are often used in spiritual and metaphysical contexts to describe individuals who are dedicated to promoting peace, healing, and spiritual growth in the world. While there is some overlap in their meanings, there are subtle differences between the two.

Lightworkers

Lightworkers have awakened to their spiritual purpose and are actively working to bring more love, light, and positivity. They are often referred to as "way-showers" or "beacons of light." Their primary role is to guide others toward a higher consciousness and spiritual understanding.

In recent years, the number of people who identify as lightworkers has been on the rise, and many believe this is due to a greater collective awakening on Earth. As we move into a new era of consciousness, lightworkers are playing an increasingly important role in helping to shift the planet towards a more positive and harmonious state.

So, what exactly is the role of a lightworker on Earth right now? Here are a few key aspects:

Spreading love and positivity
One of the leading roles of a lightworker is to spread love and positivity wherever they go. They understand that everything is energy and that their thoughts, words, and actions directly impact the world around them. By radiating love and positivity, they help to uplift the energy of those around them and create a ripple effect of positive change.

Holding space for healing
Lightworkers are also skilled at holding space for healing. They have a deep understanding of the power of energy and can use techniques such as meditation, energy healing, and prayer to help facilitate healing for others. They are also excellent listeners and can hold a non-judgmental space for others to share their stories and emotions.

Guiding others toward their spiritual path
Another vital role of a lightworker is to guide others toward their spiritual path. They understand that everyone has their unique journey and that no "right" way to connect with the divine exists. Instead, they help to empower others to find their truth and connect with their inner guidance.

Working toward a higher collective consciousness
Finally, lightworkers are working toward a higher collective consciousness for all humanity. They understand that we are all interconnected and that what we do individually impacts the whole. By working towards more extraordinary love, understanding, and unity, they are helping to create a more harmonious and peaceful world for everyone.

Light warriors
A light warrior is an individual who actively engages in promoting

Introduction

positive change, fighting against injustice, and protecting the vulnerable. Here are some everyday actions and characteristics associated with light warriors:

Advocacy: Light warriors often speak out and advocate for causes they believe in. They may use their voice, platform, or resources to raise awareness about social, environmental, or spiritual issues that require attention and change.

Activism: Light warriors may participate in activism by organizing or joining movements, protests, or campaigns to address and rectify social injustices. They actively work towards creating a more equitable and harmonious society.

Healing and Transformation: Light warriors understand the importance of healing and transformation at both personal and collective levels. They may engage in various healing modalities, energy work, or alternative practices to facilitate growth, healing, and spiritual awakening in themselves and others.

Empowerment: Light warriors empower others by encouraging self-empowerment, self-love, and self-care. They strive to inspire individuals to recognize their strengths, gifts, and potential, enabling them to make positive changes in their lives and the world around them.

Protection: Light warriors are often driven by a strong sense of justice and compassion. They actively work to protect the vulnerable, defend human rights, and ensure the well-being of marginalized communities, animals, or the environment.

Inner Strength and Resilience: Light warriors understand the importance of cultivating inner strength, resilience, and self-mastery. They may engage in meditation, mindfulness, or energy work to maintain their energetic balance and be better equipped to face challenges.

Balancing Light and Shadow: Light warriors acknowledge and work with the light and shadow aspects of themselves and the world. They recognize the need to address and transform their limitations, fears, and negative patterns while actively working to bring light into areas of darkness.

It's important to remember that the role of a light warrior is not about engaging in physical battles or promoting violence. Instead, light warriors use their energy, actions, and awareness to bring about positive change, protect others, and create a more harmonious and just world.

A light warrior takes a more proactive and assertive approach to bring about positive change. While they share the same intentions of promoting light, love, and healing, light warriors are often more actively involved in addressing and challenging the darker aspects of the world. They may actively fight against injustice, inequality, and negativity by advocating for social change, raising awareness, and taking action to protect the vulnerable. Light warriors may engage in activism, be involved in environmental causes, or work to expose and transform oppressive systems.

Lightworkers primarily focus on personal growth, healing, and spreading light through love and compassion. At the same time, light warriors combine their spiritual awareness with a more assertive and active approach to effect positive change in the world. These terms are not rigidly defined, and individuals may resonate with one or both aspects, depending on their personal beliefs, experiences, and chosen service paths. All Lightworkers and Light warriors play an essential role on Earth right now. They are helping to shift the planet towards a more positive and harmonious state by spreading love and positivity, holding space for healing, guiding others toward their spiritual path, and working towards a higher collective consciousness.

Raising Your Vibration
When I feel stuck, my vibration is usually off. Vibration is the frequency

Introduction

at which you operate physically, emotionally, and spiritually. It significantly impacts your overall well-being and the experiences you attract into your life. Raising your vibration means elevating your energy to a higher frequency, positively impacting your overall well-being. Your vibration is the energetic frequency you operate and is influenced by your thoughts, emotions, beliefs, and actions.

You may experience joy, peace, love, and gratitude when in a high vibrational state. Conversely, when your vibration is low, you may feel anxious, stressed, and disconnected. Raising your vibration involves consciously choosing thoughts, emotions, and behaviors that align with higher frequencies.

Here are a few ways to do this:

1. **Practice gratitude:** Focus on what you are grateful for, which can shift your energy from negative to positive.
2. **Connect with nature:** Spending time in nature can help you feel more grounded and connected to the present moment.
3. **Engage in self-care:** Taking care of yourself physically, emotionally, and mentally can help raise your vibration.
4. **Meditate:** Meditation can help quiet your mind and make you feel more peaceful
5. **Surround yourself with positive people:** People who uplift and support you can positively impact your vibration.
6. **Listen to high-vibrational music:** Music can powerfully impact your mood and energy levels. Listen to music that makes you feel good.
7. **Do what you love:** Engage in activities that bring you joy and fulfillment.
8. **Eat high-vibrational foods:** Eating a healthy diet of fruits, vegetables, and whole foods can help raise your vibration.

9. **Practice forgiveness:** Let go of grudges and forgive others. This can release negative energy and help you move forward.
10. **Speak positively:** Use positive affirmations and speak kindly to yourself and others.

You can improve your overall well-being and live a more fulfilling life by consciously raising your vibration.

Welcoming Solar Flares

The planet's primary way of creating this new cycle is by raising the vibration of every living thing. How does our Creator do that, you may wonder? Several methods, with one primary way of sending solar flares from the sun. The sun is a powerful force affecting our planet, bodies, and health. Solar flares are powerful bursts of energy that are released from the sun's surface. They are caused by magnetic activity on the sun's surface and can release energy equivalent to millions of nuclear bombs.

Usually, within a day or two of the release, energy sensitives, children, and animals feel them. These flares and general ascension symptoms may include: feeling jittery, exhausted, wired, tired, craving sweets, insomnia, headaches, floaty, unsettled, blurred vision, hopelessness, or agitation. They can also have a wide range of effects on our bodies, including: migraines, cardiovascular issues, sleep disturbances, fatigue, and other health problems.

Many even seemingly gain weight overnight. It's our body's way of receiving the light codes and putting on protective weight as it processes the new energies. These flares carry light codes (literally light from the sun) that enter our bodies. Connecting at our core, we receive them, take what we need, and allow the rest to filter out of us into Mother Earth while sharing with others on Earth. This is us sharing our Light on Earth!

Introduction

As I understand it, these light codes are available to every living thing on Earth. However, only some receive them. Your free will and soul contracts will determine whether or not you are open and sensitive in allowing the light code upgrades into your energy field. It doesn't matter where you live on Earth or your social status! It's available for ALL if you are open. The more solar flares and light codes you allow yourself to receive, the more sensitive you become. The flares carry light codes to upgrade your DNA while raising your vibration.

Astrologer Pam Younghans says, "Metaphysically, solar flares affect our energy fields and can initiate a process of clearing, where toxins that have been stored in the cells of the body are released. This can result in experiencing waves of sadness, anger, fear, and other lower-frequency emotions. These may manifest as overreactions to events that usually would not affect us, or they may seemingly appear on their own, with no clear trigger or source. As this clearing happens, a short-term increase in body temperature can also be felt as a hot flash."

When I first began experiencing solar flares in 2010, I would be in bed for days. It took me another couple of years to understand what was happening. Although by all appearances, I was sick, I wasn't necessarily ill. My body literally couldn't move. Even worse, I would gain weight overnight and feel like a hot air balloon ready to burst! It would take a few days to settle into my system, and my body would return to normal. It was the strangest thing. And it took me years to figure out what was going on. I needed a wardrobe for skinny, average, and solar flare days!

Although our solar flares are getting stronger and even closer together, my body has come to receive them more quickly and effortlessly. I've stopped fighting [what I resist, persists] the energy, allowing my body to accept it and process it with love. We don't want to BLOCK or fight this; we want to receive the light upgrades while reassuring our bodies it is safe.

Our physical vessel is getting upgraded with each of these bursts from the sun. The light codes sent have specific purposes while targeting the dense stuck energies in our bodies. Solar flares are classified based on their energy output, with the most potent flares classified as X-class flares. The solar flares have a scientific rating including A, B, C, M, and X, with X being the highest exposure and A the least. Then there is a number from 0-10 after the letter to rate them. So, an X Class 10 is the strongest of solar flares. These flares are measured via the Schumann Resonance.

Schumann Resonance

The Earth is a complex system with numerous interconnected parts, constantly interacting with the surrounding space environment. One of the interesting phenomena associated with the Earth is its frequency, also known as the Schumann resonance. The Schumann resonance occurs when electromagnetic waves in the atmosphere are trapped between the Earth's surface and the ionosphere. Specifically, the resonance occurs at a frequency range between 7.83 and 33.8 hertz, with the fundamental mode at 7.83 hertz being the most prominent. This frequency range is in the electromagnetic spectrum's extremely low-frequency (ELF) range and is too low to be detected by the human ear.

The Schumann resonance was first predicted by the German physicist W.O. Schumann in 1952. He hypothesized that the Earth's atmosphere would act as a waveguide, allowing for the propagation of electromagnetic waves at specific frequencies. Schumann's theory was later confirmed by measurements taken in the 1960s by a team of researchers led by Herbert König.

The significance of the Schumann resonance lies in its relation to life on Earth. It is believed that many living organisms, including humans, have evolved in a background of this frequency range and may be affected by it. Some researchers have even suggested that the Schumann resonance could regulate the body's biological clock, promote healing, and enhance cognitive function.

Evidence suggests that changes in the Schumann resonance may be linked to changes in the Earth's magnetic field and other geophysical phenomena. For example, some researchers have observed correlations between changes in the Schumann resonance and seismic activity, suggesting that it may be a precursor to earthquakes.

The Schumann resonance is a fascinating natural phenomenon that plays a significant role in the Earth's atmospheric and geophysical processes. While its precise effects on living organisms and the human body are still not fully understood, resonance remains an intriguing subject of study for scientists and a source of fascination for many people. Several websites online give you the hourly read-out of the solar flares and Earth's hertz. With each solar flare, the Earth's hertz spikes. On December 6, 2019, the highest recorded Schumann resonance was 158 Hz.

I use several additional words and concepts throughout the book that may be new to you. Below are a few of those.

Intuition

Intuition refers to the ability to understand or know something immediately without the need for conscious reasoning or analysis. It is often described as a "gut feeling" or a sense of knowing that arises spontaneously without any apparent logical or rational basis. Intuition can be influenced by past experiences, emotions, and unconscious processes and can be a valuable tool for decision-making and problem-solving. However, it can also be subject to biases and errors and should be balanced with careful analysis and critical thinking when making important decisions.

Resonance

Resonance refers to an object or system vibrating at a particular frequency that is in harmony with an external force or stimulus. When an object is subjected to an external force that matches its natural vibration frequency, it will vibrate with greater amplitude or intensity. This is because the object absorbs and stores the external force's energy, causing it to vibrate at its resonant frequency. Resonance can occur in many different systems, including mechanical, electrical, and acoustic systems, and is an essential concept in fields such as physics, engineering, and music. In some cases, resonance can be beneficial, such as in musical instruments, where it produces a rich, full sound. However, it can be destructive in other cases, such as when a bridge or building vibrates at its resonant frequency and collapses.

Energy Clearing

Energy clearing means removing negative or stagnant energy from a person, object, or space. It is based on the belief that everything is made up of energy and that negative or stagnant energy can cause physical, emotional, or spiritual blockages that may lead to problems or difficulties. Energy clearing aims to restore balance and harmony by removing negative or stagnant energy and allowing positive energy to flow freely.

Mindfulness vs. Meditation

Mindfulness is a mental state of being aware and fully present in the current moment, without judgment or distraction. It involves non-reactively focusing on your thoughts, feelings, and physical sensations, allowing you to observe them without getting caught up in them. Mindfulness can be practiced at any time, during any activity, such as walking, eating, or washing dishes. It is often used to reduce stress and anxiety, improve focus, and enhance well-being.

Meditation, on the other hand, is a practice that involves training the mind to focus and achieve a state of deep relaxation or heightened awareness. It typically involves sitting in a quiet place with eyes closed and concentrating on a specific object, such as the breath, a mantra, or a visualization. Through regular practice, meditation can help cultivate a sense of calmness, inner peace, and greater self-awareness.

Chakras

Chakras are energy centers in the human body according to ancient Indian (or Hindu) spiritual traditions. The word "chakra" comes from the Sanskrit language and translates to "wheel" or "disc." Although there are hundreds of chakras recognized, the seven main chakras run along the spine, from the base to the top of the head, each associated with a specific color, sound, and aspect of human consciousness, such as grounding, creativity, power, love, communication, intuition, and spirituality.

These chakras are believed to be connected to the body's different physical, emotional, and spiritual functions. When balanced and open, the energy can flow freely, leading to a sense of vitality and well-being. When they are blocked or imbalanced, it can cause physical, emotional, or spiritual issues. Different practices and techniques, such as yoga, meditation, and energy healing, can help balance and activate the chakras.

Aura

An aura is an energy field that surrounds living beings, including humans, animals, and plants. It is believed to be composed of subtle, luminous radiation that emanates from the body and extends beyond the physical form. The aura is composed of different layers, each corresponding to another aspect of the individual's being, such as physical, emotional, mental, and spiritual.

The colors and patterns of the aura reflect the person's state of being, including their thoughts, emotions, health, and spiritual development. Different colors are associated with other qualities and energies, such as red for vitality, blue for communication, and purple for spirituality. Various techniques, such as aura photography and energy healing, are used to visualize and work with the aura, to balance and harmonize the energy, and to promote physical, emotional, and spiritual well-being.

Religion vs. Spirituality

Religion and spirituality are often used interchangeably, but they have distinct differences. Religion refers to a formalized system of beliefs, practices, and rituals that often involve the worship of a deity or deities and a set of rules or commandments to follow. It usually has an organized structure and established institutions, such as churches, temples, or mosques. Religion often includes a community of followers who share common beliefs and practices.

On the other hand, spirituality refers to a personal and subjective experience of a higher power or divine presence. It involves an individual's search for meaning, purpose, and connection to something greater than oneself. Spirituality can be practiced in a variety of ways, such as meditation, yoga, prayer, or nature walks, and it is often a more individual and less structured practice than religion. While religion and spirituality can overlap and complement each other, they can also differ in their approach to life's big questions. Religion may provide answers and guidelines for followers, while spirituality encourages individuals to find their truth and meaning.

Expand your Consciousness

Expanding consciousness refers to increasing awareness, understanding,

Introduction

and perception of oneself and the world around us. It involves moving beyond our limited and conditioned ways of thinking, experiencing life, and exploring new levels of awareness and understanding. Expanding consciousness can involve various practices and techniques, such as meditation, mindfulness, yoga, psychedelics, or spiritual practices. Through these practices, individuals can access higher states of consciousness and explore new dimensions of reality beyond their everyday experiences.

Expanding consciousness can lead to a deeper understanding of oneself and one's place in the world, greater empathy and compassion, and a greater sense of interconnectedness with all life. It can also lead to a more profound spiritual experience, a greater sense of purpose and meaning, and a more fulfilling and meaningful life.

In the tapestry of life, we all navigate our own unique paths, some twisting like wild, burnt french fries, others flowing smoothly. No judgments here, just a diverse spectrum of journeys, each with its own pace and rhythm. The collective weight of ascension, its symptoms, and the weariness it brings are threads that weave through our experiences.

Remember this truth:

The way out of chaos is inward.

The way out of disconnection is inward.

The way out of numbing is inward.

My life, much like yours, isn't a linear trajectory of seamless events. It's a collection of decisions, some circuitous and seemingly nonsensical, that have brought me to this very moment. Each choice led me to invaluable lessons, sometimes obscured until I cleared away the clutter.

As we embark on these tales, suspend judgment and embrace a higher perspective. Together, we'll explore stories of love, heartache, joy, and moving through the rollercoaster of existence, even soaring on the eagle's perch to catch glimpses of my own cray-cray life.

Within these pages, you'll discover narratives of loneliness, generational trauma, ethereal conversations, light language, navigating shadows, and more. This book is a haven for those who've struggled to find their place, those labeled the "black sheep," or those deemed too sensitive for the world's harshness. If you seek answers amidst the shifting sands of our reality, if your high-vibrational path still feels mired in challenges, then this book is your guiding light.

The Wisdom Within: Cracking the Secrets of Meaning, Purpose, & Security offers a treasure trove of tools, from leisurely kayaking on the surface to deep-sea diving into your psyche. As our planet undergoes transformation, we're called to plunge into our inner realms. In a world of uncertainty, rest assured, life persists on the other side. Embrace this journey with me, shedding the old to make way for profound transformation. Amidst the crumbling structures, find solace in grounding yourself, anchored in your core. Within, you'll discover the meaning, purpose, safety, and security you seek. May these words be a blessing beyond measure, enriching your existence as you engage with the meditation at each chapter's close.

1

Walking Alone

Desperado, oh, you ain't gettin' no younger
Your pain and your hunger, they're drivin' you home
And freedom, oh freedom, well, that's just some people talkin'
Your prison is walking through this world all alone

~Eagles

Tears were pouring down a young pregnant mother's cheeks. She held tight onto her infant son as she waved goodbye to her new husband. He was boarding an airplane destined for his Air Force assignment in Vietnam. Before he left, though, he moved his family back to his wife's hometown in North Dakota to help with their son and the new baby.

This mother was feeling overwhelmed. Newly married and told she could never have children, she got pregnant on their honeymoon with a son. Now, quickly pregnant again and saying goodbye to her husband, any feelings of safety were long gone. On the surface, she wholly understood (as she was an Air Force nurse herself) his assignment. She began to settle into her new routine with her parents' assistance. Even so, she couldn't help but feel lonely and abandoned in addition to her already low self-esteem. She wondered if her new husband would even return alive or disabled. Would she be a single mom for her entire life?

The worries would overwhelm her while her anxiety would terrorize her. With each passing day, these emotions would accumulate. And unfortunately, these toxic feelings would feed into the baby growing in her womb.

When a woman is pregnant, her body undergoes complex changes to support the growing fetus. This includes the production of neurohormones, chemical messengers that carry information from the mother's brain to the developing fetus. These neurohormones can cross the placenta and affect the development of the fetus's brain and its future behavior and emotions. During pregnancy, a mother's emotions and thoughts can have a powerful impact on her unborn child. Studies have shown that a mother's stress, anxiety, and depression can affect the development of her fetus's brain and may even increase the risk of behavioral problems and emotional difficulties later in life.

On the other hand, positive emotions such as happiness, love, and joy can positively affect the developing fetus. This is because the neurohormones released during positive emotional states can stimulate the production of growth hormones and other beneficial chemicals that promote healthy development. "Everything the pregnant mother feels and thinks is communicated through neurohormones to her unborn child, just as surely as are alcohol and nicotine," says Dr. Thomas Verny, whose books, professional publications, and founding of the Association for Prenatal and Perinatal Psychology and Health (APPPAH) and Journal of Prenatal and Perinatal Psychology and Health, have established him as one of the world's leading authorities on the effects of the prenatal environment on personality development. Medical dictionaries define emotion as a mental and physical state, referring to the hormones and other molecules associated with emotion.[1,2]

And, "Pregnant people who had bigger fluctuations in stress from one moment to the next—also called lability—had infants with more fear, sadness, and distress at three months old than mothers with less stress variability, "reports a new Northwestern University study that examined how a child's developmental trajectory begins even before birth."[3]

It was 1967 and the height of the Vietnam War. The baby in that mother's womb was me. I was six months old when my dad saw me for the first time. Looking back on how I entered life, I can easily see where this deep well of loneliness and abandonment began. For decades, I have carried around this open gaping wound like a hole in my heart that nothing from the outside could ever fill. And trust me, I've tried everything to jam this sucker full, so I didn't feel so awful! While busy numbing myself and attempting to shove the pain down further, I continued to attract what I was. I continued to draw to me that which needed healing. I attracted those with a soul wound to which I could plug in. I also drew to myself repeatedly circumstances and events allowing for lessons. Over and over until I embraced the hurt, the hole, and allowed for healing. Dr. Michael Lennox says, "You can't heal a wound unless the wound is triggered."

Loneliness and abandonment can be difficult emotions to grapple with. It can make us feel like no one cares about us or that we are not worthy of love. These feelings can be pervasive and may impact our overall well-being. In addition, if we continue to carry these emotions in our energy field, we may attract more of the same. Our energy field, also known as our aura, comprises our thoughts, emotions, and experiences. It is like a magnet, attracting people and situations that match our energy. If we carry feelings of loneliness and abandonment in our energy field, we may attract more experiences that make us feel lonely and abandoned.

For example, if we constantly think that we are not good enough for love and attention, we may attract partners who reinforce this belief by treating us poorly or not giving us the love and attention we crave.

Similarly, if we feel abandoned by friends or family, we may continue to attract situations where we feel left out or unwanted.

Here I am, five decades later, still healing layers of loneliness and abandonment. Events, circumstances, and people continue to be thrown at me when I least expect it to cause me to feel lonely, left behind, not fit in, rejected, and unworthy. Over and over and over. Rinse and repeat, until the next layer is ready for healing.

I remember my aloneness when I crawl into bed at night, and no one is beside me. I remember my aloneness when I wake up to an erringly quiet house. It's a debilitating feeling that overwhelms me, especially when traveling, and no one on the other side of the phone wants to know that I've arrived safely. After an event, I say goodnight to everyone while watching them happily go home to their loved ones. I take a deep breath, and often with tears, am grateful that I can serve in whatever way I did and ask myself—

What's wrong with me?

What did I do to deserve this aloneness?

And it doesn't matter whether you are single or partnered. We can be lonely with constant companions near us. I felt alone most of my marriage, surrounded by dozens of friends. I thought my ex-husband needed to be home more to make me feel safe and secure. I thought it was his job that I did not feel lonely, abandoned, or worthy. In actuality, it's not anyone's job but my own.

My ex-husband spent an excessive amount of time at the office. He will be the first to admit that. Of course, as most men say, they do it for us to provide for us. I would say, "I do not mind that you work 70 hours a week, but we need to find a way to stay connected." He answered, "I can't do two things at once." I felt like I was married to a stranger. I needed more time with my husband. To me, time equals love. Therefore, I concluded that if he didn't have time for me, he didn't love me. He wasn't around to fill the empty hole in my heart as I thought he should. It would be years later before I realized that:

No one is responsible for my happiness except me.

No one is responsible for what I am attracting except for me.

No one is responsible for filling the empty hole in my heart except me.

I later learned, too, nothing outside of me—no person or pacifier—can fill that deep well inside of myself.

The strangest thing was also occurring while I desperately sought to fill my loneliness hole. I became an expert at keeping everyone at arm's length. I'm fully aware of my energy sensitivity which unconsciously keeps people away. My body is in full protection mode, pushing people and energy away that may harm me. The further out people are, the easier it will be for me to run if I feel threatened. I grew up hearing the messages that I'm too sensitive, emotional, not enough, and too much simultaneously, creating more confusion. In Chapter 6 there is an entire chapter on being highly sensitive and how I turned what I thought was a curse into a blessing.

I grew up with the verbal message from my parents, "I love you," attached to the message, "Go away." Although confusing as a child to comprehend, it was easy to continue into my adulthood. For years I would strangely push my husband and others away when they would hug me. I didn't realize what I was doing. I see now I was sending people out—physically and emotionally. I surmise the loneliness I was holding in my cells subconsciously and energetically pushed others further from me, allowing my loneliness to continue.

The concept of the Law of Attraction has gained significant popularity in recent years, with many people discovering the power of manifestation in their lives. This principle states that we attract what we focus on, and that the energy we put into the world determines our experiences. While this idea may seem abstract or even a bit woo-woo, there is a scientific basis for it, and it is based on the concept of energy and frequency.

Everything in the universe is made up of energy, including our thoughts and emotions. When we have negative thoughts or feelings, we vibrate at a lower frequency and are more likely to attract negative experiences into our lives. On the other hand, when we have positive thoughts and emotions, we vibrate at a higher frequency, and we are more likely to attract positive experiences.

This is why it is so important to be mindful of the energy we are holding and the thoughts we are thinking. If we want to attract more abundance, joy, and love into our lives, we need to focus on those things and hold the energy of those things. This means letting go of limiting beliefs and negative self-talk and replacing them with positive affirmations and gratitude.

It was a beautiful Sunday morning in Northern California. Being new to the area, on most weekends, I would take short day trips to a different location to explore. This morning I had chosen to go to a nearby mountain town, El Dorado Hills. My adventures usually begin at the town's Farmer's Market; I use my intuition to guide me from there. Today was no exception. Except I felt off. Even with all my quiet time and connection to Spirit earlier in the morning, I felt particularly lonely. I suspect the two lonely songs on the radio should have been my first clue of the energy cocktail of the day I'd be dealing with!

Walking down the street at the Farmers Market, I notice the smiling faces with people laughing as they connect to their loved ones. It's like I'm floating invisible between groups of people who don't see me. I smile, and no one looks at me. I ask myself, "Am I even here?" They continue happily communing with their groups while I wade through the crowd. On the other side of the market, I turn around and do the same, returning to my car a little sadder.

My next stop on my adventure is a coffee shop with my laptop in tow. I write these chapters while watching people come and go. Men, women, and children bustling around me. I feel like I'm in their way while their voices carry over me, making me think I am invisible yet again. This happens to me at the gym as well. Most everyone has their headphones on, with few people connecting. Although I do not miss the days when gyms felt like a singles' meat market, it would be nice if people could acknowledge each other again. Earbuds may be convenient for us to tune into our electronic devices, and at the same time, they shut us off from the world around us.

In hindsight, it's easy to see how the convergence of loneliness, abandonment, low self-esteem, sexual abuse, health issues, and child of alcoholic wounds converged into a perfect storm that only an implosion would resolve. Traditional counseling in my 30s helped resolve some of the trauma. I moved past the deeper issues when I started to do energy and shadow work in my 40s, recognizing the various stuck emotions and patterns.

Ever wonder why you struggle with something over and over? You thought "it" was gone. That addiction. The illness. The craving. How do we heal from these deep holes in our psyches? Experience it again, layer by layer. For me, go around the roundabout of loneliness to heal and clear yet another layer of deep emotion. Sometimes it can make you looney tunes when you pray, and it goes away but returns with a vengeance. You begin to doubt and question all that is. Instead of fighting, I'd like to invite you to dive in. Dive into whatever it is for you. What does it want to teach you? How can you love this part of you that you may not like? Recently, I've been diving into a chronic illness (multiple auto-immune issues and more) that has been quite debilitating over the years.

I've tried ignoring it, and that didn't work.

I've tried talking about it, and that didn't work either.

I know what I focus on expands, and what I resist persists. And, most importantly, what we love —softens and releases.

When we dive into our deepest wounds and the most significant challenges, we show love to the part that needs it the most. Rumi says, "The wound is the place where the light enters you." I remind myself daily that this illness will not stop my purpose. It's part of my purpose. Experiencing loneliness won't stop me from my purpose; it's part of my purpose.

I'm sure you will agree that this is easier said than done on many days! The illness is a gift. This aloneness is a gift. With its many layers, I've learned so much about myself, different healing modalities, the power of the mind, and more.

In the meantime, I continue to:

Acknowledge it, love it, and allow it to be.

Receive the lessons it wants me to learn.

Realize that loneliness is me—alone. Me being all-ONE with myself.

Although I consider myself quite outgoing, I am the queen of climbing into my hermit shell. I know that all of this current loneliness and what I'm attracting is my own doing. No, I do not blame my parents, kids, or ex-husband, and it's my responsibility to shift it. Regardless of how something showed up in my energy field or my subconscious, I am the only one with the power to transmute it. How empowering is that to know that you can change what's in your life?

Taking responsibility for your energy and practicing self-awareness is essential. Pay attention to how you feel in different situations and around other people. If you notice that certain people or situations drain your energy, limit your exposure to them. If you feel like you are holding onto negative emotions or experiences from the past, seek help from a therapist or energy healer to release them.

The energy we hold is what we attract into our lives. By focusing on positivity, practicing mindfulness, surrounding ourselves with positive people and experiences, and taking responsibility for our energy, we can attract more abundance, joy, and love into our lives. Remember that you can create the life you want, starting with the energy you hold.

Daily, I know what energy I send into the world around me. That's why my morning routine of resetting my energy field is of utmost importance for me and the people I encounter throughout the day. Sometimes, I need two or three more "resets" throughout my day, depending on how many people I've been around or what emotions I'm processing. And even though I may think I had a connected, perfect meditation to set my frequency high in the morning, my Guides and Angels may have felt like this was a perfect day for a pop quiz in

Earth school. I suspect they are saying to themselves, "Let's see if Lara is ready to move on from holding loneliness in her energy field. Let's throw her a few more events and see if she's triggered."

In the past, if I had a day like the few I described above, I'd be curled up in a ball, crying and asking myself, What's wrong with me? That question (and other negative ones like it) only leads to feeling worse about myself. Each negative thought would take me down a rabbit hole fit only for Alice in Wonderland. If I do not quickly notice the negative story I'm telling myself, stress continues to build in my energy field. I can feel lethargic, cranky, and crave sugar or caffeine. Although that still happens on occasion, I'm better at catching myself.

So, how can we break this cycle of attracting more loneliness and abandonment? The first step is to become aware of our thoughts and emotions. We can do this by practicing mindfulness and paying attention to the thoughts that come up when we feel lonely or abandoned. Once we know our thoughts and emotions, we can challenge them. We can ask ourselves if our beliefs are true and if the evidence supports them. We can also work on developing a more positive and self-affirming internal dialogue.

In addition, we can work on building healthy relationships with ourselves and others. This means setting boundaries, communicating our needs, and surrounding ourselves with people who uplift and support us. We can also engage in activities that bring us joy and fulfillment, such as hobbies or volunteering.

Today, my self-awareness radar is on 24/7. I stay tuned into my body, thoughts, and soul's messages throughout the day. Ideally, as soon as I feel off, I do a reset meditation to a higher vibration, like the one I've shared below. I get to choose what I'm going to believe. I can choose what I think about and what frequency I want to vibrate. Ultimately, regardless of what hand I was dealt in life, I can shift it to a more positive experience.

Now It's Your Turn!

Scan the QR Code below to hear Lara guide you through a deep light language meditation to clear energies that you may have taken on in the womb. Have a pen and paper ready to journal your thoughts.

Scan me

2

Family Traditions

Stop and think it over
Try to put yourself in my unique position
If I get stoned and sing all night long
It's a family tradition

~Hank Williams, Jr.

Growing up with generations of alcohol abuse made its mark on a young soul. I knew what a "scotch on the rocks with a twist" was long before I was in school. Although my dad drank daily, I never remember him drunk or out of control. On the other hand, my mom constantly struggled with the demons of alcohol, cigarettes, and health issues. At 5:00 pm every day, a drink was poured in the kitchen. When it came to refills, we kids were the wait staff.

Being a child of alcoholics, one of my superpowers was that I could read the room like nobody's business. Every minute, my unconscious job was to read my parents' emotions, and based on how they were feeling, I would go to "work." My job was to keep peace at all costs. Happy parents meant there wouldn't be any yelling, and I wouldn't get in trouble. At four years old, I was screamed at for not anticipating that the dishwasher needed to be emptied. I was the second oldest and oldest daughter, with four siblings in total. I learned to heat canned soup for breakfast for the other kids and other household duties. Paper plates became my friend for easy cleanup. Peanut butter and jelly sandwiches were a full meal. Sadly, I never seemed to meet my parents' high expectations. I felt like I disappointed them at every attempt. There was always something that I missed. I seemed to create more messes as I soon learned from a vile temper that soup wasn't a breakfast food.

My Spirit was broken early on. My soul began to break into fragments and return to the heavenly realm for safekeeping. Unbeknownst to me, I was now walking around, fragmented and afraid. My nervous system was always in overdrive, anticipating raised angry voices while I learned not to trust, not feel, and not speak. This created a massive disconnect with my own body. I couldn't tell you my favorite anything. I didn't have a clue.

"The family environment into which a child is born has a profound and long-term effect on the relationships that are formed by that child as an adult. Growing up in a dysfunctional family (one where alcoholism or drug addiction, sexual abuse, or neglect is present), where many of the child's basic needs are not met, does make a difference whether that child leads a productive and satisfying life. A dysfunctional family is unable to provide a safe and nurturing environment where basic trust is experienced. Children raised in dysfunctional families have difficulty developing emotionally and socially. Three rules, often unspoken, that govern families where alcoholism is present are:

1. Don't trust.
2. Don't feel.
3. Don't talk.

Children of parents with alcoholism learn at a young age that their emotional and sometimes physical survival depends upon understanding and following these rules. As adults, they often fail to recognize that these rules are unnecessary and unhealthy outside of the family's alcoholism. They don't trust others, since they learned they couldn't count on others. They seldom speak their true thoughts; instead, they say what they believe others want to hear. And they blindly maintain a tight rein on their feelings – if they know their feelings. The rules of childhood survival become a noose that squeezes the life out of an Adult Child of an Alcoholic (ACA) during adulthood—unless they overcome the menacing power of their dysfunctional family."[4]

Growing up in a household with a parent or parents who struggles with alcoholism can profoundly impact a child's life. While each child's experience is unique, some common patterns can be seen in children of parents with alcoholism. Here are some things that children of parents with alcoholism learn:

> **Self-Blame:** Children of parents with alcoholism often blame themselves for their parent's drinking. They may believe that if they behaved better or performed better in school, their parent would not drink as much.
> **Fear:** Children of parents with alcoholism may live in a constant state of fear. They may fear their parent's unpredictable behavior, violence, or abuse. This fear can be so overwhelming that it affects their ability to concentrate, learn, and form healthy relationships.
> **Lack of Trust**: Children of parents with alcoholism may have difficulty trusting others. They may have learned that promises are not always kept, and people are not always honest. This can make it difficult for them to form healthy relationships and build a support system.
> **Emotional Instability:** Children of parents with alcoholism often experience a rollercoaster of emotions. They may feel sad, angry, or anxious one moment and then happy or relieved the next. This

emotional instability can make it difficult for them to regulate their emotions and may lead to problems with mental health later in life.
Codependency: Children of parents with alcoholism may feel responsible for their parent's wellbeing. They may take on the role of caregiver and feel that it is their job to keep their parent safe and happy. This can lead to a pattern of codependency that can be difficult to break later in life.
Difficulty with Boundaries: Children of parents with alcoholism may have trouble setting boundaries. They may have learned to ignore their needs and desires to avoid conflict or keep the peace. This can make it difficult for them to establish healthy relationships later in life.

It's important to note that not all children of parents with alcoholism will experience all of these patterns. However, these patterns are common and can have a lasting impact on a child's life. Lucky me, I struggled with all of these symptoms and more.

If I'm being honest, as a teenager, I wanted my mom to drink. Generally, she was nicer when she was drinking. We could get away with more! There was a fine line, though. You didn't want to be around her if it got crossed. Not necessarily because she would be mean, just all up in your business. I was also a terrible liar so I would over-share about my life and friends. Unfortunately, she usually remembered the next day and held it against me. I felt awful and betrayed often.

One such time, I was a sophomore in college at Butler University, living three hours away from home in my first apartment with a roommate, Stephanie. She was a ballet dancer and under immense pressure to keep her figure perfect. Yet, daily she smoked cigarettes, drank alcohol, and ate loaves of bread in one sitting. Her fingernails, teeth, and hair were not only unhealthy for someone who was only 19, but falling out. Over and over, I would hear her go into the bathroom and turn on the shower like she was taking a shower, yet she never did. She'd come out just like she had gone in there. DRY. I was baffled and began to ask her questions. One day she broke down and explained to me that she was bulimic. Bulimia is an emotional disorder involving distortion of body image and an obsessive desire to lose weight. Bouts of extreme overeating are followed by depression and self-induced vomiting, purging, or fasting.

I wanted to be a good friend to my roommate, but this was WAY beyond my scope. One evening during Happy Hour, my mom called when Stephanie was away. I confided in my mom about her secret in hopes my mom would be able to give me some advice in supporting her. Instead, she held that secret for about a day and called during the next evening's Happy Hour when I wasn't home (before individual cell phones, and we had one landline phone at the apartment). Mom started drinking early and called specifically to talk to Stephanie about her struggles. I was devastated. Now, I had a roommate who was mad at me whom I saw every day and a mom I couldn't trust with any information whatsoever. Stephanie and I didn't even make it through our year's lease. Her illness got worse, and eventually, she left college. She never forgave me for telling my mom, and I struggled to understand how my mom could do such a thing to me.

A few months later, my boyfriend (and future husband) and I were returning to Indianapolis from our monthly visits to our hometown in Northern Indiana. The more my mom drank, the harder it seemed to affect me. On the car ride home, I asked by boyfriend, "Do you think my mom drinks too much?" I will never forget him looking at me and saying, "Lara, everyone knows your mom is the town drunk. It's okay. She is so loved, and she is a wonderful person, and she struggles with alcohol. My mom told me about her when we started dating. And it's okay."

Well, this was ALL NEWS TO ME! I was furious with him for telling me about the pink elephant in the room. You don't know the difference when you live with this every day. Only when I had some distance in college did I understand the enormity of the situation.

Soon after, I dove into addiction books, counseling, and anything that would help me better understand my mom's demons and why I was the way I was. Guilt plagued me everywhere, even if I didn't do anything wrong. I suffered from debilitating low self-esteem, while my self-hatred was immense and grew with each passing day. I felt I had to constantly prove myself to anyone who would listen, even momentarily. I was crying out for help, and no one seemed to hear me, least of all myself.

My siblings and I attempted to do an intervention on at least one occasion for my mom, and our dad stopped us before it even got scheduled. He knew she needed help, and he wasn't about to be the bad guy and have to live with her after we had all gone home. I'm not sure which was worse for my dad, taking the alcohol out of the house or putting up with decades of verbal abuse because of it. We will never know. And we all had to respect and honor my dad's wishes on this. Other dear friends also offered help and were shut out of my parents' lives if they mentioned the drinking.

Life continued to unfold as it did. I noticed that anxiety would overtake my body if there was an upcoming family event or holiday. I would be sick suddenly. Shaking, nervousness, and even vomiting seemingly out of nowhere would overtake me. After having children, visits home to my family grew even worse. Growing up, I knew I had no choice in how I was treated when alcohol talked, but I always thought I could protect my kids. It wasn't long before I realized that wasn't true, either.

We were making our way from Indianapolis to Northern Michigan

Family Traditions

for a week-long summer family vacation. Our first stop was at about midnight in our hometown. Mom and Dad knew we were coming in late that night, so they left the front door unlocked for my husband, my boys (ages 7 and 9), and myself. Our oldest son ran into the house, and I was behind him. What we saw as we entered etched a vision I will never forget as long as I live.

My mom was lying in a pool of blood on the couch, and I was uncertain if she was alive. It looked like she had been stabbed, as blood was everywhere, even on the floor and furniture. After letting out a huge scream, my husband took the kids immediately upstairs while my dad and I attended to her. She refused to go to the ER, so we put her in the shower to wash the blood off and see where she hurt herself. There was a large gash on the back of her head, and her nose was bleeding simultaneously. We were able to bandage her the best we could.

Everyone was happily sleeping by the time I got upstairs. On the other hand, I was shaking, crying, and vomiting. My body was attempting to process what the heck had just happened. I'm sure I slept a few hours that night, but the following day was the kicker. When I came downstairs, the blood had already been cleaned up. My mom was sitting at the kitchen table reading the morning paper while my dad was outside with the sprayer hose washing away the blood-stained deck where my mom had fallen the night before. There were no signs of any disarray other than my body still trembling.

I began to ask questions and was told it was none of my business. My mom wasn't bleeding anymore, although her entire face and eyes were already beginning to bruise. My dad washed away any evidence of foul play while attempting to sow self-doubt and confusion in my mind that it had occurred at all.

I indeed doubled down on counseling after that incident, learned about gaslighting, and continued working on myself being a child of alcoholics. According to numerous articles published on adult children of alcoholics, they often: [5]

- Find it difficult to maintain relationships
- Feel inadequate and insecure
- May be impulsive
- Become hypervigilant
- Suffer from PTSD or anxiety disorders
- Struggle to regulate emotions
- Have a fear of abandonment
- Difficulty forming intimate bonds
- Have a fear of change
- Have feelings of inadequacy

I have experienced all the above and learned to avoid conflict and maintain peace at all costs, even at my own expense. I could be impulsive, judgmental, overreactive, inconsistent, self-isolating, and more. At a very young age, I learned not to speak my truth, that my feelings don't matter, and that whatever I thought was WRONG. It's a wonder, as messed up as I felt, that I could lead a relatively everyday suburban life, or so I thought!

My mom wasn't a bad person. She was the most loving person I knew — to others. She hated herself and didn't know what to do except numb herself. It was not a priority for her generation to be taught tools to heal their hurting hearts. Later in life, my mom's drinking began to turn on her even more. Aside from all the physical health issues she endured, emotionally, she was deteriorating as well. She became paranoid about people talking about her. Passive-aggressive, narcissistic behavior was now the new normal. We walked around on pins and needles. I never knew if what I said would trigger her into a verbal attack or storming out. I would devise any excuse I could to avoid a family get-together.

I do not doubt that my trauma from living in such an unstable household affected me much more than I may ever know. I'm apologizing ahead of time to my children, who suffered the consequences of my low self-esteem and perceived inadequacies. After decades of sitting in the church pew and studying my unique brand of energy work, I began to see the role generational curses played in my life. Generational curses are patterns of negative behaviors, energies, or outcomes passed down from one generation to another within a family. These can affect a person's life, such as finances, relationships, health, and mental well-being. In some cases, they can be traced back to specific events or traumas in a family's history.

When I was first single, I began to attract quite an array of new friends, many with some addiction to drugs or alcohol. It bewildered me that this was even happening. I knew, in general, what I am, I attract. As I began diving deeper into my inner work, I saw that even though I didn't necessarily have their specific addiction, I was carrying a similar soul wound in my energy field from my generational lineage. Some ancestral vows and traditions were at play, affecting me unknowingly. The energy-sensitive types, like myself, and most likely you, if you are reading this book, will understand that you feel and hold others' emotions. This realization opened a new world as I was shown how to clear such addictions, vows, agreements, and more. At the end of this chapter, I invite you to join me in following along in a generational curse/pattern clearing.

I was shown that clearing specific layers of curses, vows, addictions, and habits with energy work in myself would also set my ancestors free generations BEFORE AND AFTER me. How amazing is that? The work I do, and YOU do, heals the generations before and after us. We are invited to do our inner work to stop the madness of issues holding our loved ones back from being their highest and best. Suppose you notice a repeating pattern, belief, self-serving tradition, vow, addictions (alcohol, smoking, gluttony, laziness, porn), or anything that is repeating in your lineage. In that case, you can shift this direction for YOUR ENTIRE FAMILY. Just because it happened in the past doesn't mean it has to go with you in the future. You are invited to participate in an ancestral clearing of blockages at the end of this chapter.

Deuteronomy 28:15–68 alone contains 53 verses listing generational curses. A few of the symptoms of curses are listed here:

- Poverty
- Hereditary disease
- Divorce
- Child abuse
- Sexual abuse
- Domestic violence
- Alcoholism
- Drug addiction
- Depression
- Confusion
- Fear
- Indecision
- Panic attacks
- Mental illness
- Suicide
- Destructive attitudes and behaviors

While identifying and breaking generational curses can be challenging, it is possible to do so with intention and spiritual practices. Here are some steps to break free from generational curses and create a positive legacy for future generations.

Family Traditions

Recognize the patterns: The first step in breaking generational curses recognizes the negative patterns passed down in your family. This requires a deep level of self-awareness and reflection. Take time to think about the patterns you've noticed in your life and how they may be connected to your family history.

Identify the root cause: Once you've identified the patterns, it's essential to understand where they originated. This could involve researching your family history, talking to older relatives, or seeking guidance from a spiritual advisor or therapist. The goal is to gain insight into the events or traumas that led to the negative patterns in your family.

Release the past: To break free from generational curses, it's essential to release the past and let go of any negative emotions or beliefs holding you back. This can involve forgiveness, meditation, or energy healing practices such as Reiki, EMDR (*Eye Movement Desensitization and Reprocessing*) or EFT (Emotional Freedom Technique).

Create a new narrative: Once you've released the past, creating a new narrative for your life and your family's future is important. This involves setting positive intentions, affirming your values and beliefs, and taking action to create the life you want to live. This could include setting goals, creating a vision board, or working with a spiritual coach or mentor.

Practice self-care: Finally, it's important to prioritize self-care as you work to break free from generational curses. This could involve regular exercise, eating a healthy diet, getting enough sleep, and practicing mindfulness or meditation. When you care for yourself, you'll be better equipped to break free from negative patterns and create a positive legacy for future generations.

Breaking generational curses requires courage, self-awareness, and a willingness to do the work necessary to create a better future. By recognizing the patterns in your life, identifying the root cause, releasing the past, creating a new narrative, and prioritizing self-care, you can break free from the negative patterns that have been passed down in your family and create a brighter future for yourself and your loved ones.

As difficult as my childhood was centered around alcohol, I loved my parents dearly. There wasn't anything I wouldn't do for them, sadly, even at the risk of my own health and family peace. These stories aren't meant to hurt or embarrass anyone in my family. My parents have since transitioned into their Heavenly bodies. And, while I hear from them often in the Spirit world, I certainly feel their presence as I write this chapter. They support my work and encourage others to clear their generational energies to be set free.

Dedication I wrote and read at my mom's funeral 3/17/17

As I prayed about what I was going to say this morning to honor Mom, many years of love, laughing and tears came to mind. Her generous and giving spirit overflowed into whoever she encountered. She never knew a stranger as she was instant friends with new acquaintances.

Mom was certainly a one-of-a-kind, no holds barred woman. Often honest to a fault.

She had some silly sayings that we will never forget.

For example, "Whatever makes your socks go up and down."

Horse feathers.

"Uff-duh" is another one... I still don't really quite know what that means!

Another one... "We're off like a herd of turtles in a cloud of pickle dust."

Family Traditions

And

another favorite...

"Pi-shaw" (which essentially means shut-up). A few of her friends heard that one more than once!

When she was physically able, Mom knew how to enjoy life to the fullest and was quite resourceful. She planned several themed parties for their friends and for us, camping trips. On one such camping trip when were much younger, Steve, Brian, myself, and family friend Tracey Brook, got our shoes all muddy and wet while out playing. This was our only pair of shoes for the weekend so needless to say Mom wasn't thrilled with us. When it came time for dinner, she opened the electric skillet, and our shoes were in there to our dismay! She told us we were having SHOE SOUP for dinner!

Mom went out of her way to help those in need. We kids watched and participated with her in her yearly American Cancer Society Daffodil Days deliveries. We also tripped over walkers, toilet seats, and wheelchairs she stored, managed, and delivered to hospice patients in DeKalb County. On many occasions, we were blessed to go with her on the delivery of the equipment in need. I personally would watch her hold the hand of a dying patient encouraging the person in their last days of life. Undoubtedly, it was not a coincidence that her life ended with hospice as her support team.

Her heart to help others poured out whenever she physically could.

All too often, though, overwhelm would set in. Nevertheless, Mom was a survivor. She battled depression, anxiety, breast cancer, a house fire, life challenges, physical pain, emotional pain, and inner demons that wouldn't stop. During the last decade, she endured as best she could. Regardless of her state, she often reminded us kids how much she loved us.

I was in town just a few weeks ago and spent a lovely evening with Mom and Dad. When I left that day, I knew it would be the last time I would get to talk to her. Many things went through my mind...

How much I love her. How much I will miss her.

But mainly, I was in awe of my parent's unending love for each other. Married almost 52 years, Soul mates committed to each other till death do they part. They demonstrated a love that grew even while the body was fading.

We will never forget her courageous and persistent spirit. Her fight for a quality of life amid challenging circumstances.

And, this morning, as sad as we all are for losing our mom, we take comfort in knowing she is finally out of her pain... as stated in

Revelation 21:4

He will wipe every tear from their eyes. There will be no more death or mourning or crying or pain, for the old order of things has passed away.

Client Story: Mary

Mary, a client who has had her fair share of health issues since childhood, hired me to dive into her family's history of well-being. What we found quite interesting was a pattern of puzzling illness running through the women and children in her family. Oddly enough, the men in the family seemed to dodge most of it.

Embarking on a journey that transcended time, I traced

the threads back three generations on Mary's maternal side, eventually arriving at her Great Grandfather. As was sadly common in that era, I was shown that he had taken land from the Indians. The act of appropriation had reaped a heavy toll—the Chief's pregnant wife and their other children were casualties of the ensuing turmoil. This catalyst compelled the Chief to interweave his resentment into the very fabric of the lineage, ensnaring the women and children of Mary's grandfather within the web of a generational curse. He vowed they would have slow, mysterious health issues that would cause them to suffer greatly.

The narrative took a profound turn when Mary's ancestral lineage, fueled by a deep sense of remorse, sought reconciliation. A dialogue that transcended time and space ensued as they humbly sought forgiveness from the Chief, the very figure who had cast the curse. Astonishingly, the Chief, embodying the essence of forgiveness and understanding, extended his benevolence. The shackles of the curse were unshackled, and the lineage was set free from the clutches of its age-old torment.

As this story of reconciliation spread through time, things shifted for Mary and her family. The women and children in the family dealing with health issues began to gain clarity while the majority of the ill members getting better over the next few months. Hidden potential for healing runs deep in most family's history if time and attention are given to reviewing the past for the impact on the present.

Now It's Your Turn!

Scan the QR Code below to hear Lara guide you through a deep light language meditation to clear generations imprints. Have a pen and paper ready to journal.

Scan me

3

She Talks to Angels

Says she talks to angels
Said they call her out by her name

~The Black Crowes

My fascination with angels and the higher dimensions began at a young age. As a child, I had an imaginary friend, John Peeker, who was always by my side. I didn't feel safe unless he was with me. Although invisible to the naked eye, John was as much a part of my life as any other human friend. My mom would set a place for him at the dinner table, and my siblings were instructed to make room for him in the car. I don't remember much about John besides feeling safe when he was with me. He was my confidant and friend—an extension of myself, yet separate.

We would communicate in light language. Although not understood in the human sense, my heart received the messages. In addition to speaking the language of light, I would also write him notes in light language, which looks like Egyptian hieroglyphs. For more details on light language, go to Chapter 12, where I've written extensively on this unique subject.

At the time, I didn't comprehend what I was saying or even what light language was. I knew we had a secret communication that calmed and comforted me. I wanted to do nothing more than hang out with my invisible friend and connect in our secret language. I couldn't see him with my naked eye nor hear him with my physical ears. Yet, I knew when he was present and when he wasn't. I could feel his love for me, hear him (telepathically), and on occasion, see the outline of him through my 3rd eye.

Children having imaginary friends is not new. Lauren Young, writing for ScienceFriday.com, says, "Imaginary companions are much more common than people might think. Up to two-thirds of children have them, typically between the ages of 3 and 8."[6]

According to Eileen Kennedy-Moore, PhD writing on Psychology Today, "Having an imaginary friend is not evidence that a child is troubled. However, imaginary friends can be a source of comfort when a child is experiencing difficulties. There are many case studies of children inventing imaginary friends to help them cope with traumatic experiences."[7]

The summer I turned eight years old changed my life forever, after repeated sexual abuse incidents by trusted family friends. I began to have numerous health issues, including recurring bouts of mononucleosis, ear infections, and bloody noses while crying myself to sleep almost every night. I lost my zest for life, while shutting down my communication with John and my ability to communicate with light language. With my steady friend gone now, I felt incredibly alone in the world. My parents didn't know what to do about my crying every night, as I couldn't voice what I was experiencing.

I didn't feel like I belonged anywhere, especially within my family. I felt like an alien who had been plopped down on the wrong planet. One summer, I insisted that my mom show me my birth certificate to prove I was part of our family. To make matters worse, she could not find my birth certificate, thus fueling my feelings of insecurity and estrangement. Decades later, my birth certificate appeared, although a little too late to reassure a scared little girl.

Even without my imaginary friend, some form of spirituality was always my deepest passion. I didn't want to miss church when I was a little girl, as I received something special there that helped me through the week ahead. My grandparents often took me to the Auburn Presbyterian Church in Northern Indiana. When I could drive myself, I would meet my grandparents on the pew, volunteer, acolyte, and was quite involved in youth group. I felt like an outsider and misfit; however, at church, near Spirit, I felt an unexplained belonging.

Fast-forward to my 40s, I was glued to my couch with a chronic illness and grieving a divorce. I wasn't attending or volunteering at church regularly any longer; yet during this time of solitude, I began to meet God for real and commune with my higher self, guides, and angels. I let go of people-pleasing and began to say no more often. I released what I thought the perfect life should look like and was grateful for the many blessings in front of me. I forgave myself for hurting those whom I loved so dearly. I would sit silently (for about a year) in prayer, meditation, and writing. Angels would appear, my imaginary friend returned, and light language became my constant companion again, grounded in healing and love. I came to understand that John was one of my guardian angels.

God was ever so present in my life like nothing I had ever experienced. I wasn't chasing or working to please God or others; instead, I was being. I could soak up God's love, peace, and healing in the stillness.

Day by day, my body would release stuck emotions and trauma. This time in stillness was healing and allowed an opening to the Heavens that I had never experienced before, nor did I know was even available. I began to see, hear, feel, and know unique angelic presences and Spirit energy in its purest form. I would channel light language as well as auto-write messages. Their messages were always cheerful, loving, and helpful.

I talk to the Great I am, God, Source, Spirit, Universe, Creator, Divine Mother/Father, whatever name you use for your higher power, every day and throughout the day. My angels, archangels, guides, higher self, and specific ascended masters also hear from me simultaneously. I make it a habit not just to talk, but also to listen intently. Prayer, for me, is when I'm doing the talking, and meditating is when I get quiet while listening to guidance.

My guides all have an energy they emit that tells me who they are and what their purpose is. Some have specific names and some don't. I do not get caught up in their actual name. We humans want to label everything. If it helps you to ask for their name, please do. I want to know who someone is and their energy, regardless of their name. I am very particular about what energy, what angel(s), and what spirits I allow into my life. At first, I would talk to whatever angels or spirit guides showed up. I was being bothered at all hours while it seemed every Tom, Dick, and Harry wanted to chat with me. If they appeared, I thought I had to be the one to talk to them or help them — often to my demise.

At this same time, my elderly mother-in-law lived in assisted living near us. I would visit often and interact with other residents as well. For several weeks I was awakened by different residents in the middle of the night. I would see their smiling faces with no apparent body and recognize them from the assisted living facility. They wouldn't say anything, and although they seemed happy, it was beginning to freak me out! After three different residents appeared, and within a couple of weeks, all three passed away, I started to ask questions of my spirit team. From what I was told, these particular residents, as with many people near the end of life, go in/out of the spirit world several times and sometimes for months before they make the complete transition. If they are afraid, they come and go often until they feel comfortable. A quick hello in an elevator to a resident connected them to my calming Spirit. They ventured in and out of their light as they slept and saw mine nearby.

I also had supernatural visits from a high school ex-boyfriend detoxing in rehab, my father-in-law, who had just passed, and several others I didn't know by name. It was quite an experience! I believed I had to talk to them because they contacted me. As time passed, I became more discerning with whom I allowed to talk to me from the other side of the veil. Soon, only those highest frequency angels, spirits, and guides came through.

Just because they are in Spirit doesn't mean they are better or know better than you. Sometimes their job is to confuse, sabotage, or distract you. The lower-frequency beings often look for a light to guide them. Yes, even across the veil, a soul can be lost or unable to find their way to the light. You may be the shining light, like a moth to a flame, that they see. Trust yourself and your inner guidance, especially if they left Earth too soon or abruptly. If something feels off, it most likely is.

This brings me to a topic I've never heard talked about before. We can have a spirit on our Spirit Team that isn't helping us! The energy could be…

Great-grandma or any deceased relative who loves you and wants to help you but doesn't understand your purpose in this lifetime.

A spirit disguises themselves as love and light to get you off course by giving bad advice.

A confusion, distraction, distortion, or trickster energy that is being used to derail you.

And, not as often, but I have seen other persons' spirits attached to people. This is quite complicated as you are whole and complete, yet deceased energy has glued to you. No matter the reason, you have agreed to it at some level. Many of these energies have been with people since birth others come in later in life.

When Spirit created the light, the dark was also created. In addition to discerning who comes through from the Spirit world and their intentions, we must understand that much darkness on Earth is being disguised in the light. Before hanging out with them, we must know other people's energies and purposes. Always keep your BS meter on! We are not always safe at church or among so-called spiritual people. And, just like in real life—toxic, low-frequency friends will show up. The question isn't if—it's when. And what will we do with them? And, at what cost to ourselves? I had to learn how to block these new toxic friends whose only motive was to bother or distract me for their selfish reasons. You are in charge. You can tell your Spirit Team who you want to chat with. It's your choice! Own your energy and own who comes into your energy—on Earth and spiritually.

Recently I was abruptly awakened by the snake-like energy of a friend coming at me whom I had talked to the evening before. We hadn't chatted in years, and just a brief conversation on the phone reconnected us at an energetic level. Although he spoke all love and light, his energy said something completely different. Being human as I am, I ignored it, talked to him anyway, and went to sleep happily, thinking about how we had made plans to see each other in a month. However, when I awakened, what I saw and felt energetically from him coming at me was pure evil. An energy was moving through him that wanted to distract, sabotage me, and take me down.

I can always tell when I'm getting ready to up-level; I am tested in many ways. This was just one of the pop quizzes of the week! Will I see this person even though I know it's not the best choice for me? What he is saying is exactly what I want to hear, but underneath the words is evil energy. People can say all the "right things," but if you tune into your gut and something feels off…run! Trust that you may be duped.

The dark elite is using many conscious and heart-centered people during this time of awakening. Especially the sensitive, empathic types who are around many people. Such as the case of my friend. They are soaking up others' energy and weakening their systems, allowing for an accessible entrance of even more infiltration of dark powers. The dark energies have an agenda of evil and to stop anyone pure at heart from spreading love and light.

In addition, many popular spiritual teachers who are shining bright get their power from something other than the highest frequencies. If you took the time to read their energy, you would see dark powers running them, especially from the heart chakra area. In the next few years, spiritual teachers with any selfish, greedy, alternative or dark motive will be revealed. And at the same time, many others hiding in the shadows doing their inner work will rise to the top seemingly overnight. Do not be surprised at this switch. Welcome the new higher resonance with pure-hearted teachers.

Everyone is on their journey. It's not for us to judge. However, we must choose who we will allow to be on our journey with us. Whom do you want to play in your sandbox? Discernment is of the utmost importance as we move forward within this unique new earth landscape.

I began praying immediately after being awakened and shown the truth of the situation with my friend. My stomach, my power center, was hurting immensely, so I started by sending back to him any energy coming from him into my solar plexus. I felt like he was trying to weaken my power, hence the direct attachment to my power center. Convincing me to do something I knew wasn't right — meeting him for a rendezvous. Then I tore up and burned (in my mind with intention) my soul contract with him. As soon as that was complete, his dark energy came at me even stronger over the next couple of days. This often happens as they feel disconnected from you and want you even more! This energy was vile and evil, and I was encouraged to put my entire energy field in a beautiful bubble of love and protection and surround myself with a wall of burning fire. As the energy he was spewing was coming at me, it was burned up immediately. I never slept so well!

The interesting thing about this man is that he's being used for evil purposes and has NO idea. It's not up to me, unless asked, to clear him or help him see what's going on. It is up to me to own my energy while protecting myself and my family. And to be very clear on who I will let into my life. Along with the prayers and energy work around releasing that friend from my life, I had to take action in the physical. After contacting him to cancel our future meeting, I blocked him on my phone—end of discussion.

Trickster Energies

Recently there have been some strange happenings in my house. One afternoon, I was sitting on the couch when a slipper flew off the high coat rack. Aside from getting my attention, oddly, I couldn't find the second slipper—until a week later. It was upstairs in my closet. Hmmm, I thought. The next day, I was looking for something I had left on the kitchen table. And, yet, it was nowhere to be found. I looked for an hour, walked back to the kitchen table, and there it was. Hmmm,

I thought. I had just climbed into bed and heard my razor fly across the shower. Hmmm, I thought. Late one evening, two days later, my friend and I sat on the couch discussing the day. All of our computers were off, yet somehow, my printer in another room turned on and began to act like it was going to print. It went on for about 30 seconds, then finally shut off. Hmmm, I thought.

When something like this occurs, my first ask is, are there any evil, dark energies in my house? I continued to hear "NO." And, honestly, there weren't. The house felt great. Yet, something was off. What could it be? I go through the checklist in my head:

- Malevolent, dark energies
- Distraction, distortion energies
- Ghosts
- AI/Holograms/Alien
- Flying Monkeys
- Disturbed nature energy
- Indigenous native energy
- Leprechauns ~ trickster enemies

Bingo! It was the last one. The leprechaun is principally a roguish trickster figure who cannot be trusted and will deceive whenever possible. Every couple of years, these little bothersome pests show up. If things feel off for you, use my list above and double-check your energy field and house.

As soon as I realized what sort of energy I was dealing with, I prayed, asking for my home to be cleared of this particular energy. And, immediately, all the odd happenstances ended.

Angels

From what I understand intuitively, we all have one primary guardian angel. Often there are several more as well, who are with us throughout our soul journeys to assist, guide, and protect. To me, angels are God's voice and hands in action. Angels appearing and talking to people is nothing new, and is mentioned many times in the Bible. Although not a complete list, below are a few facts we know about angels from the Bible.

> **We know God created angels.** In the New Testament, Paul tells us that God created all things "visible and invisible." According to Scripture, they're part of the universe God created.
>
> **There are three types of angels.** Scripture names three categories of heavenly beings that appear to be types of angels: cherubim, seraphim, and living creatures.
>
> **Angels have a hierarchy.** Angels in the Bible appear to have a rank and order. In Jude 9, the angel Michael is called an "archangel"—a title that indicates rule or authority over other angels.
>
> **Only two angels have names in the Bible: Gabriel and Archangel Michael.**
>
> **Angels carry out some of God's plans.** Angels are God's voice and hands on Earth, from delivering messages and judgments, giving God glory, patrolling the Earth, providing protection, and more.
>
> **Angels are very powerful.** Angels are called "mighty ones who do his word" (Psalm 103:20), "powers" (see Ephesians 1:21), "dominions" and "authorities" (Colossians 1:16).

You may ask yourself, "Why do Angels talk to Lara?" I don't know, other than I'm open to it. I'm not any more special or not than anyone else. Everyone on the planet can have God, their angels, and their guides talk to them if they are open to hearing from them. There is no reason to be resentful or jealous that others see/hear from these fantastic spiritual beings or speak in light language. You can too! I will include a meditation at the end of this Chapter for you to call in and be open to your angels, specifically. I suspect billions of people on the planet are now communicating with God and their Spirit Teams.

As mentioned, I call out to the Creator, my angels, and guides every morning. Most days, I feel their presence and hear their guidance with ease. On other days, it's crickets. Where did they go? Why can't I hear, see, or feel them today? The sun shines behind the clouds on a rainy, cloudy day, yet we cannot see the sunshine. And, like the sunshine, my Spirit Team is seemingly hiding behind a veil more so than on other days.

When we first open up this new higher realm, like a toddler learning to walk, they hold our hands with each step until we get the gist. Soon though, they let go to encourage us to strengthen our walking muscles. They are nearby, watching and ready to catch us if we fall. Later, they push us out of the nest to fly alone. There's no reason to be angry for being pushed out of the nest; it's a necessary step in our soul growth.

Although I do not believe they are not male or female per se, their energy may feel predominately masculine or feminine, and sometimes even neutral sexual energy.

What are some things you can ask your angels for? Anything! Some of my daily responsibilities my guides and angels help me with —

> Traveling safely
> Parking spots
> Moving help
> Clear traffic
> Stay motivated and organized
> Special projects
> Help for family members
> Find missing items

Stand guard while I'm sleeping for physical and spiritual protection
Turn the food I eat into a high vibe for my body
Move stuck energy
Archangel Gabriel - to speak clearly and get a message out

The following angels and guides are my go-to for assistance with daily work of energy clearing while protecting myself and my family:

Archangel Michael
Archangel Metatron
Archangel Gabriel
Archangel Raphael
Mother Mary and Jesus and of course, Our Creator of the Universe

Travel

Before I leave on a trip, I call upon Archangel Michael and his legion of warrior angels to help clear the energy of all planes, trains, automobiles, and hotel rooms I'm about to encounter. I pray that all transportation runs smoothly, safely, and is on time. I pray that I, all passengers, and the vehicle I am in are put in a white tunnel tube of love and light safely going from one destination to another.

I read the hit book **Hiring the Heavens** by Jean Slatter many years ago. The tips from her book came in handy with all my moves around the country, as I call in my Moving Angels. When I sense another move coming on, I call upon my Moving Angels, who want to assist me in finding the highest and best next home and city. I specify my criteria and always add on at the end, "Or something better!"

In many respects, our spirit friends are the same as our physical friends. They like to be acknowledged, and they like to spend time with us. They want to have two-way communication with us. And, just like our physical friends, if we ask for something with a grateful heart, they can sense our appreciation and want to be there for us even more.

One crucial aspect of our Spirit friends is remembering that because we have free will, they cannot interfere unless a dire situation requires their invention. For example, if we are in a car accident and it's not our time, our angels can assist instantly. Otherwise, imagine your angels, guides, and a vast spirit team of loved ones standing by while watching you fall off your bike, yet unable to help. Their hands are tied until you ask for assistance or guidance. Unless it's not your time to leave this Earth or God has asked them to intervene, they must honor our free will. Always know they want to assist and are always on call for you, especially if you ask with a grateful heart.

As I left the gym yesterday morning, I saw a man driving erratically in my rearview mirror. He was swerving over several lanes with a near miss of me by a few inches. Immediately, I called upon my angels for help. I didn't even get much past yelling "ANGELS HELP" when the driver took a quick right turn away from me, across three lanes, and up the curb to knock off a tire. Although he kept going, I could tell he was being guided away from me. I continued to pray that he would get stopped before he hurt someone. I do not doubt that supernatural assistance was close by for me. The more we communicate with our guides and angels, the closer they are, and even faster they act on our behalf, especially regarding protection.

It's the Christmas season with long lines at all postal facilities. I had one package left to mail; however, each time I stopped at UPS, Fed EX, or USPS, the lines were out the door. I'm now on a writing retreat in a strange city. I went to bed last night asking my angels to guide me when and where would be the best place to mail my package with the least amount of waiting and the best energy. My other request as

I was drifting off to la-la land was that I would love to know a little breakfast cafe the locals frequent.

After eight hours of uninterrupted sleep (not), I woke up with a message to get going. It was 7:58 a.m., and I drove across the street to the UPS store opening at 8 a.m. When I arrived, four people were already in line, then myself, and ten others behind me. I had a wonderful conversation with a retired Marine during my short wait. I didn't get to walk right in without a line, but I'd like to know if any angel could arrange that this time of year! I left the UPS store feeling fulfilled that the package was on its way to my daughter-in-laws, that the angels had guided me, and that I got to talk to a happy someone in line.

The next stop this morning was—COFFEE! You probably know by now that I love me an excellent local organic coffee shop. However, this morning, I was led to a Starbucks right off the highway. Usually, my first response to going somewhere I don't want to go is, UGH, seriously? I get weary of having a place built up for me to visit, and it ends up being an energy shit-show of clearing transmutation with me being the trash can. I write in detail about this in Chapter 7. Regardless, here I sit at Starbucks with my non-organic extra mold, chemical, and additives drink!

All that to say, while I was sitting here, I overheard a lady reading an email out loud (which was annoying me) to her husband from their granddaughter, who lives in the city I was visiting. She was reading out loud the best little local breakfast cafe to go to! My prayer was answered, although not how I thought it could have been!

The two main things I've learned over the years, sometimes in excruciating ways, are that I can ask and believe, but the HOW and WHEN are up to God. I am laughing at HOW my request for a little breakfast cafe showed up. That was a new way to tell me! I like that my guides are getting more creative with me. These are just a few examples of how my Spirit Team guides me daily. Interestingly enough, sometimes, I am not led how I believe I should be led.

For months, when I would pray, asking for guidance on where to go for community and friends in this new area I was living, I intuitively heard to go to Crate & Barrel at the mall. Seriously, shopping? You don't have to tell me twice to do that! It was right next to the gym where I work out, so it was easy-peasy to run in. I made about four trips before I put my foot down and told my guides this was ridiculous. I wasn't meeting anyone and just bought a little something each time. I am often led to do something or go somewhere that seems silly, like the Crate & Barrel experience. There are different reasons for each, but suffice it to say, none of the expeditions were accidents. There were always teaching moments for myself or someone I encountered that needed a smile. It may have differed from the light and love event I desired, but that doesn't mean it was wrong or I misheard my guidance. I have no doubt it was perfect.

The odd guidance often wears me down while teaching me to be unattached to the outcome, and just because I think it should be one way doesn't mean it is God's way. I cannot see all the puzzle pieces, especially regarding my own life. When it does happen, it teaches me:

- To trust myself, the Creator and my Spirit team
- To stay unattached to the outcome
- To have discernment on who is speaking/guiding me
- The importance of staying connected, talking to your team/friends in person while keeping toxic weeds out of your life

Interestingly enough, this Chapter was challenging for me to write. Communing with the higher dimensions is such an integral part of my everyday life, like brushing my teeth, that I had trouble remembering what life was like before them! They are the foundational piece of who I am. I would be lost without their leading, guiding, supporting, and loving energy. They are my constant companions and are always available. Sometimes they even wake me up in the middle of the night to chat! Seeing, hearing, knowing, and feeling them is so typical that I too often brush off their presence and their magical miracles as commonplace. I am ever grateful for their constant friendship and guidance. They never turn me away, they greet me with a smiling face, and are encouraging yet honest and loving.

Now It's Your Turn!

Scan the QR Code below to hear Lara guide you through a deep light language meditation to meet your spirit team. Have a pen and paper ready to journal.

Scan me

4

Words are Energy

"Words are spells and hold an energy that is alive. Words are not just combinations of letters; they carry energy that can profoundly impact us and others. They hold the power to inspire, uplift, and heal, but also to harm, wound, and destroy."

~Lara Jaye

If there's one thing the world's pandemic taught us, it's that life is short. We are only here on this earth for a brief time. What is it that you desire to do? What is it that your soul is craving? The only way to know is to become more self-aware. And to become more self-aware, it takes time—time alone getting to know yourself, what makes you tick, and healing those parts of you that get triggered. Much of this work involves giving up our numbing devices of choice so that we can feel whatever emotions are screaming to come to the surface. Instead of running to the kitchen for a spoonful of ice cream or a shot of tequila, sitting in the uncomfortableness of what is speaking to you takes practice, patience, and grace with ourselves.

That is truly the foundation for living the most amazing life ever. It's about getting to know yourself and falling in love with yourself as you are. Accepting and loving those parts of you that may seem less than what you think they should be is the most beautiful thing you can do for yourself. You may have heard the saying, "What we resist persists. And, what we focus on expands." We only enlarge the issue when we consistently tell ourselves we are not worthy or not enough. The opposite is loving ourselves. When we show love to something or someone, they soften. This is the exact opposite of resisting. They soften and allow.

I've struggled with body dysmorphia since I was a child. Body dysmorphic disorder (BDD) is a condition where a person spends a lot of time worrying about flaws in their appearance. These flaws are often unnoticeable to others. People of any age can have BDD, but it's most common in teenagers and young adults, affecting both men and women. People with body dysmorphic disorders often check themselves in mirrors because they believe they have physical flaws. Or, like me, they do the opposite and avoid mirrors, photos, and videos altogether! Growing up, I had cardboard over the mirror on my dresser so I didn't have to see myself. I remember prom night, peeling back the cardboard to see if my dress was on straight.

In my first book, **More Than Enough: Discover Your Limitless Potential & Live Your Bravest Dream**, I detailed the "enough" message that plagued me and many of our generation. I never thought I was good enough, had enough, was doing enough or ever thin enough. I believed I would only be successful in any area of life if the scale said what I thought it should say.

No one would love me if I weren't thin enough.

No one would hire me if I weren't thin enough.

No one would be my friend if I weren't thin enough.

Interestingly enough, recently, I did weigh and look like how I so dreamed of. And guess what? The number on the scale didn't matter one bit!

It seems so silly to keep talking about this in my 50s. However, it's clear that as an adult, I am still making occasional unconscious decisions based on my early childhood imprinting and other unhealed traumatic occurrences that have happened along the way. Unless we are self-aware and take time to heal those unprocessed wounds, we will continue to be triggered or make a choice that isn't in our highest and best. I see my body dysmorphia arising from various sources. I do not doubt I was born with some of my mom's insecurities. And, with the wound already open, I was an easy target for teasing including being told I was fat and ugly. This just added to my not feeling good enough.

Regardless of the relentless teasing, I felt great about myself the summer I turned 14. I had thinned out (from not eating) and was already fully grown in height at 5' 5" and 125 lbs. The summer sunshine and sparkling pool in our backyard were my haven and happy spot. This particular day was unusual because my mom joined me in the pool. I seldom remember her ever getting in the water. She usually enjoyed it from afar with a beer or scotch in hand. This day though, she swam up to me leisurely, laying on a floaty, and began to tear apart my body. She was telling me how fat I was. She grabbed one of my thighs with both her hands and said, "Look, how fat this is! It's bigger than an Easter ham." Over and over, body part by body part was made fun of. Telling me, I needed to be on a diet and lose weight. Looking back on that memory, I can easily see that she was projecting her unresolved emotions onto me. At the time, though, I felt belittled and ashamed.

What is a PROJECTION?

Imagine, if you will, a projector on our head, looking out into the world. As we are all walking around, we are projecting our "stuff" onto others. It may show up as the other person being rude or selfish as they talk demeaningly to you. In reality, you are acting as a mirror. What they are saying, they are saying to themselves. What we see in others mirrors ourselves.

Projection is a theory in psychology in which humans defend themselves against their unconscious impulses or qualities (both positive and negative) by denying their existence in themselves while attributing them to others. For example, a habitual person may constantly accuse others of being rude—sort of a blame-shifting.

Projection is quite common in everyday life. It's a clue to how we are doing or what we need to work on. It mainly happens when we have many unprocessed emotions we don't want to deal with. We may be numbing ourselves to hide from unprocessed emotions. Eventually, though, it's going to show up. It may show up as anger projected onto someone else, usually those closest to us—our loved ones.

It's also important that, before we blame others for being a certain way or complaining about so-and-so being selfish, we need to look within. These uncomfortable, embarrassing, and frustrating emotions we don't want to deal with will appear. According to famous psychologist Sigmund Freud, these emotions are projected onto other people so that other people become carriers of our own perceived flaws. Fortunately (or unfortunately) for us, this form of emotional displacement makes it much easier to live with ourselves because everyone else is responsible for our misery, not us. We are the victim or the good and righteous person.

There's no end to the types of feelings or emotions we can project onto others, but here are a few of the most common:

1. Insecurity or Body Image Issues

When we feel insecure about some aspect of ourselves, especially our body image, we often project onto others those same insecurities. For example, they are so ugly. In reality, you think you are ugly or whatever you call the other person, and you are probably just insecure about yourself. People with low self-esteem tend to put others down because that's how they feel about themselves. This is what bullies often do. And this is precisely what my mom was doing in the example above.

2. Attraction to Someone other than your partner
   This is quite common when someone is attracted to a third person. They feel it's unacceptable to be attracted to someone else, so instead, they blame their spouse for cheating. It's their way of not dealing with their feelings.

3. Disliking someone
   They don't like me. If you dislike someone but you aren't willing to admit it, you may try to convince yourself that the other person doesn't like you. In reality, you don't like her but are unwilling to admit your feelings.

4. Anger
   Anger is a widespread feeling that is often projected onto others. You may be steaming on the inside, but instead of handling it yourself, you tell yourself so-and-so is such an angry person.

If you notice that you are being triggered by something or someone, I invite you to look closer inward. We all project in our daily lives to protect ourselves against emotions, thoughts, and perceptions that we judge as being too bad, ugly, shameful, or even uncontrollable. If you feel someone is projecting their unresolved hurts onto you, telling them isn't ideal. Holding up the mirror to them most likely will be met with massive resistance and reactivity that you think you're all that and a bag of chips. This is a time in your life when you should lay down your desire to be correct and focus on yourself.

Even when I haven't asked, many times I've been the target for people to tell me what they think I should be doing differently. I find this very intrusive, and always have to check myself. When am I giving unsolicited advice? A good rule of thumb for us all is to keep our opinions to ourselves unless asked point blank. People ask questions when they are ready to hear the answers. So, save your energy! Let's honor that we are all on our soul journey, and learning is optional! Projecting thoughts or emotions onto others allows you to consider how dysfunctional the other person is, without feeling uncomfortable knowing that these thoughts and feelings are your own. Thus, we can criticize the other person, distancing ourselves from our dysfunction.

This is one of the problems with projecting our unresolved wounds onto others—it makes us think we are superior to others. I don't have to look at my inadequacies if I can see your flaws. Instead, I can focus on how messed up you are! It made my mom feel better to tear apart her 14-year-old daughter so she didn't have to look at her open wounds. We fail to see the good in people because we are so busy picking out others' flaws. In reality, they are our flaws!

Secondly, projecting can create a mess because we don't deal with our feelings in the first place. Managing our emotions is something that should be taught at an early age. Instead, we learn how to stuff and numb them as fast as possible. What if we welcomed our feelings to rise to the surface for release? Set aside our fear of them and allowed them to be. It's then, and only then, they can't hurt you anymore. Until dealt with, the unprocessed emotions become the trigger that we use to wound others, especially those we love the most.

We must become aware of what we're doing to stop projecting onto others or reacting. It's about getting quiet, being still, and noticing what's happening in our lives. What are we saying to the people around us? What are we saying to ourselves?

When you see others in a negative light, ask yourself, "Am I projecting?" Also, understand that when others put you down, they may be projecting criticism of themselves. We must all know the energy and emotions we're beaming into the world.

When I was separated from my husband, I felt emotionally and physically sick most days. I would sit on my couch, staring out the window, and dream about a happier life ahead. I was incredibly depressed, unhealthy, and feeling awful. One afternoon, a gal from our church curiously asked me about my plans since I was getting divorced. I blurted out that I loved the southern coastal area near Encinitas and Carlsbad, California. To paraphrase her response with kinder words, she clarified that I wasn't thin enough to live there! She said it was a different lifestyle than what I was accustomed to in Indiana, and in her opinion, I wasn't the cookie-cutter Botox model that would fit in coastal Cali.

I was speechless. Unbeknownst to me, she had moved her family to Indiana from that exact area. Again, looking back, it's easy to see that she was projecting her inadequacies and insecurities onto me. She was in the fitness industry, and apparently, the burden of being thin and perfect via Cali standards was a constant pressure cooker for her.

I had just shared the pinnacle location I wanted to live and was told I wasn't good enough, thin enough, or enough in any way shape or form to even think of living there. Her words reflected the pain she carried every day in her heart. The pressure to conform into that lifestyle was too tremendous and unattainable for her. Regardless of why she said what she said, I know that I've moved all over God's green earth

Words are Energy

EXCEPT that area because I didn't believe I was good enough. And, in my weakness, I received her words into my consciousness almost as a mandate that I could never move to that area. And, because it was already an open gaping soul wound for me, her ill words stuck. If I didn't already have a similar trauma imprint, it probably wouldn't have made much difference. It would have washed right off like water over a duck's back.

Words are spells and hold an energy that is alive. Words are not just combinations of letters; they carry energy that can profoundly impact us and others. They hold the power to inspire, uplift, and heal, but also to harm, wound, and destroy. The energy of words is often underestimated, but when we understand and harness their power, we can use them to create positive change in our lives and in the lives of those around us.

Words are energy in that they carry vibrations and frequencies that can affect our thoughts, emotions, and even our physical well-being. Words emit energy that can be felt and experienced, like sound waves or electromagnetic waves. This is evident in how certain words can evoke strong emotions, such as joy, love, anger, or sadness.

On the DailyOM,[8] they write, "Each word we use has a life of its own, a vibratory signature that creates waves in the same way that a note of music creates waves. And like musical notes, our words live in communities of other words and change in relation to the words that surround them. When we are conscious of the energy behind our words, we become capable of making beautiful music in the world. If we are unconscious of the power of words, we run the risk of creating a noisy disturbance."

Positive words, such as "love," "kindness," "gratitude," and "hope" carry high frequencies that can uplift our spirits and create a sense of joy and inspiration. When we use these words daily, we can spread positive energy to others and create a ripple effect of kindness and compassion. For example, a simple "thank you" or "I appreciate you" can brighten someone's day and make them feel valued and acknowledged.

Furthermore, the words we speak to ourselves profoundly impact our self-esteem, self-worth, and self-confidence. The internal dialogue we have with ourselves shapes our beliefs, perceptions, and actions. When we use positive words to affirm ourselves, such as "I am capable," "I am worthy," and "I am enough," we boost our self-esteem and empower ourselves to achieve our goals. However, when we use negative self-talk, such as "I am a failure," "I am stupid," or "I can't do it," we diminish our self-worth and limit our potential.

Many of us have experienced praying for someone and hearing from them acknowledging they thought of you or felt your prayers. Prayer is mighty because it's such a focused intention of words, thought, and emotion, usually wrapped in gratitude. The person you are praying for often thinks of you or feels an extra touch of love.

And the opposite of prayer is a negative-focused intention of thought and emotion. We feel those as well. The saying "sticks and stones may break my bones, but words will never hurt me" is dead wrong. Words DO hurt, both physically and energetically. And, have you ever "felt stabbed in the back?" I have been awakened from a deep sleep feeling someone's deep energetic stab in my back. Words are an energy or vibration directed at someone (or yourself) and can create a spell. The word "spell" actually influenced the idea of using magic to influence others. Spell is derived from the (before) 9th century word "spel," which meant magic, charm, influence, magical powers, and fascination.

Negative words, such as "hate," "criticism," "blame," and "judgment" carry low frequencies that can lower our vibrations and impact our mental and emotional well-being. When we use these words thoughtlessly or intentionally, they can hurt others and create a toxic atmosphere. For instance, hurtful comments or derogatory remarks can leave deep emotional scars, damage relationships, and lead to conflicts and disputes.

Even our Creator knew the power of speaking words. Genesis 1:3-25 NLT Then God said, "Let there be light," and there was light.

So, how can we use the power of words to help rather than hurt?

1. Practice mindful speech: Before speaking, take a moment to reflect on the words you are about to use. Are they kind, uplifting, and optimistic? Will they inspire and encourage others or hurt and bring negativity? Choose your words carefully and speak mindfully to create a positive impact.

2. Cultivate empathy and compassion: Words can be powerful tools for empathy and compassion. Listen actively to others, acknowledge their feelings, and respond with kindness and understanding. Use words that show empathy, such as "I understand," "I'm here for you," and "I care about you." Such words can provide comfort and support to those in need.

3. Use affirming words: Be mindful of the words you use to talk to yourself. Replace negative self-talk with positive affirmations. Encourage and uplift yourself with words of self-love, self-acceptance, and self-empowerment. For example, "I am capable," "I am worthy," and "I can do it."

4. Resolve conflicts with mindful communication: When faced with disputes or disagreements, choose words that promote understanding, collaboration, and resolution. Avoid blame, criticism, and harsh language that can escalate the situation. Instead, use words that express your thoughts and feelings assertively and respectfully.

5. Share words of appreciation and gratitude: Express your gratitude.

Now, the energetic implications of jealousy and envy aren't pretty. When others talk about you and are jealous, they appear as daggers, usually in the back area. Sometimes they are tiny daggers, and unfortunately, others are large. Often, they look like hooks as well. It depends on how intense the feelings are attached to the words. These are invisible daggers, invisible energy, and yet they can cause physical pain and heaviness. It may feel like an overall heaviness (if there are a lot of daggers) or a sharp, stabbing feeling. It can keep you in a negative mind loop while making you feel off-balance.

You could also be sending these daggers or hooks out to others. Where do you feel intensely jealous, envious, judgmental, or hateful? Perhaps you were talking about someone the other day with intense emotion? Those words leave your mouth and enter their energy field, which is bee-lined directly to and attached to them. They might have even felt it enter them if they were sensitive.

Jealousy and being envious of others are interesting energies. There is a profound message in it if you allow yourself to go there. Dive deeper into why you feel jealous. What is it about them you are jealous of? Are they living the life you desire? I suspect that if you are jealous of an aspect of someone's life, then you have that desire inside of you to do that as well, yet you aren't living up to your full potential. You may not have stepped into your full expression of yourself, yet. Observe this in your own life and see where you are not living the life you know you are capable of. We wouldn't be jealous of people we don't care about ever having something they have or do.

Whether spoken aloud or in your psyche, words have a vibration that can either encourage and breathe life OR do the opposite. This is exactly what happened to me in the stories above. Although my mom or my church acquaintance may not have meant ill will, their words left their mouth, entered my energy field, and attached to an already weak, damaged wound. I soaked their words as a spell, confirming and solidifying that I was not good enough or thin enough.

I'm sure, like me, you have spoken ill of others and received the daggers of deceit. At any time, you can repeat the Ho'oponopono—an ancient Hawaiian practice of reconciliation and forgiveness. While envisioning the person or circumstance in front of you that is heavy on your heart, repeat these four sentences with intention.

I am sorry.

Please forgive me.

Thank you.

And I love you.

Repeat over and over until you feel the energy lift and the universal laws of forgiveness take effect.

It's so important to recognize how powerful our words are. Words are energy and create intentional spells. What kind of energy do you want to send and receive in return? What words have people spoken to you that you held onto? We should all strive to live by the golden rule: "Do unto others as you would have them do unto you."

Now It's Your Turn!

Scan the QR Code below to hear Lara guide you through a deep light language meditation to clear psychic daggers and imprints. Have a pen and paper ready to journal your thoughts.

Scan me

5

Mind Games

> We're playing those mind games together
> Pushing the barriers planting seeds
> Playing the mind guerrilla
> Chanting the Mantra peace on earth
> We all been playing those mind games forever
> Some kinda druid dudes lifting the veil
> Doing the mind guerrilla
> Some call it magic the search for the grail
> Love is the answer and you know that for sure
> Love is a flower you got to let it grow

~John Lennon

I don't know about you, but sometimes my mind can take me on a ride like no other. The twists and turns of my imagination, intuitiveness, the energy cocktail of the day, and sometimes a not-so-positive perspective sets me back a few notches. Mastering the monkey mind has been one of my biggest challenges, and I'm making significant progress in it, even if it isn't perfect. My motto with most things is PROGRESS, NOT PERFECTION!

Our minds can certainly play tricks on us, and may even persuade us to believe we are unloved and unworthy. If we allow Negative Nelly in our head to lead us, there is no telling what dead-end road we will encounter. On the other hand, if we take control over our thoughts, we could be living the most amazing life ever!

How do we know what is true? In the silence of the night, a passing thought may tell us a defeating, negative view, or an uplifting, favorable position on the same subject. Which is true? And how does confirmation bias play into this mind game?

Confirmation Bias can control and even sabotage us. According to the American Psychological Association, Confirmation Bias is the tendency to look for information that supports, rather than rejects, one's preconceptions, typically by interpreting evidence to confirm existing beliefs while rejecting or ignoring any conflicting data. Confirmation Bias is the tendency of people to favor information that confirms their beliefs or hypotheses. Confirmation Bias happens when a person gives more weight to evidence that confirms their beliefs and undervalues evidence that could disprove it.[9]

People display this bias when they gather or recall information selectively or interpret it biasedly. And, the Universe will always desire to show us we are RIGHT, so we may only see that evidence. The effect is more substantial for emotionally charged issues and deeply entrenched beliefs. This explains what is currently happening in the U.S. political arena, with few seeing each other's viewpoints, let alone respecting the difference of opinions. Social media algorithms also duplicate this, showing us only what we initially were drawn to.

As Catherine A. Sanderson points out in her book ***Social Psychology***, confirmation bias also helps form and re-confirm our stereotypes about people. Sanderson CA. Social Psychology. 1st ed. John Wiley and Sons; 2010. "We also ignore information that disputes our expectations.

We are more likely to remember (and repeat) stereotype-consistent information and to forget or ignore stereotype-inconsistent information, which is one-way stereotypes are maintained even in the face of disconfirming evidence.

Combine Confirmation Bias with the fact that, as a human, studies show we naturally tend toward the negative. Mastering the monkey mind can be challenging, and negative thinking is a typical human trait. Well, that explains a lot! Especially if the generations before us tended to be more negative-minded. It takes much more work on our part to be positive and smile.[10]

Humans have an average of 50,000-70,000 thoughts per day. According to Brookhaven Hospital, as many as ninety-eight percent of these thoughts are the same as the day before. Even more significant, eighty percent of our thoughts are negative, which drains our energy. Begin to pay attention to your thoughts. Once you notice negative thoughts running in the background, you can CHOOSE to change them. First, you must start with awareness. And, to get the awareness, you usually need a quiet area with the TV/music off.

Numerous studies have proven that a chemical reaction sends messages throughout our body for every thought we think. Negative thoughts are particularly draining. Thoughts containing words like "never," "should," and "can't," complaints, whining, or ideas that diminish our own or another's sense of self-worth, deplete the body by producing corresponding chemicals that weaken the physiology. No wonder we're exhausted at the end of the day! Dr. Bruce Lipton says, "The work shows that your mind's perception of the world changes your biology, the chemistry of your body, which changes your cells."

Imagine your mind as a radio receiver. Each channel is programmed to play something completely different. One channel may focus on negative thoughts, complaining, or gossip. The next track over may be the 'NOT ENOUGH' channel. "I am not enough, I am not doing enough, and I don't have enough" channel. My thoughts get stuck on that channel all too often! The next track over on the dial doesn't make any sense. It sounds like words my friend would repeat. I was picking up her channel now too. And, yes, we pick up thoughts from people we know and the collective in general. It will take effort and focus on turning the dial even further to hear encouragement from Spirit or to tune into those channels that bestow positive messages. Those channels are harder to tune into, but once you do, Shazam!

The messages you allow to play in your head is always your choice. Those messages, whatever they are, aren't only silent words. They create chemicals that pulsate through your body and give your cells detailed instructions on how to feel. How you feel determines how you will act. The good news is that if you recognize a negative or limiting thought, you can consciously change it before it derails you!

When going through my most challenging time years ago, I intuitively knew that if I began sending positive messages to my body, it would eventually reflect that positive image. Often dread would come over me regarding an upcoming event. I would start to feel listless, tired, angry, and even frustrated thinking about what could happen. As I began noticing the negative thoughts, I would reframe them to envision my ideal outcome. I would focus on the best-case scenario, not the worst. It wasn't long before my mood began improving with a brighter outlook. With each reframing of the negative thoughts, my energy magically increased. The chemicals produced by my body as a response to these positive messages were much more likely to support me.

Daily complaining, comparing, and negative thinking will bring us exactly that. Happy people, you guessed it, get happier in their life. Unhappy, sad, grief-stricken folks attract more of the same. If that isn't enough reason to watch your thoughts, I do not know what is! Have you ever noticed that it expands when you focus on something? This phenomenon can be seen in many areas, from relationships to careers to personal growth, and it is the idea that what we focus on expands.

When we focus on something, we give it energy and attention, which can attract more of the same into our lives. For example, if we focus on positive aspects of our lives, such as gratitude and abundance, we may attract more positivity and abundance into our lives. On the other hand, if we focus on negative aspects, such as fear and lack, we may attract more negativity and scarcity. The energy we put into the world is what we attract back to us. So, if we focus on positive things, we attract more positivity, and if we focus on negative things, we attract more negativity.

What we focus on expands. So, if we're focusing on...

> I do not like where I am in life.
> I do not like my work.
> I don't make enough money.
> I hate my body.
> There is never enough. I am not enough.

Not only does your body "hear" your thoughts, but corresponding chemicals are also sent straight to ALL your cells throughout your entire body. The Creator of the Universe also hears you as you speak these honest yet low vibratory words.

If you're focusing on what you do not have, that is exactly what you will get more of. When we struggle or feel stuck in life, we only see what keeps us stuck. Negative Nelly takes over. It takes much more work to see and believe something different than what has always been or is in the moment. It can be more challenging to get in the emotion of it, especially if we desire something different in our lives that we've never experienced before. In order to shift to a new reality, though, we need to begin acting as if. Our focus needs to be on higher vibe.

This isn't about faking it until you make it. Nor is it essential to be Polly Positive when you're truly depressed. What is important is to acknowledge where you are and to call in how you want to feel. See Chapter 11 for details on Jumping Timelines. The concept of "what you focus on expands" also does not mean we should ignore or suppress negative emotions or experiences.

I've been in the depths of depression and took antidepressants for over a decade while weekly counseling held me steady. Do whatever you need to do to support yourself in finding the silver lining each day. My mind has played every trick in the book on me. It's been an ongoing struggle to stay positive amid life's challenges. I am determined to find the joy in life, which means watching my thoughts and all that I allow into my energy field. I know how amazing I can feel. And anytime I feel off, I slow down, reassess my thoughts, and go through my energy-clearing steps. It is about shifting my focus to the positive and cultivating a more balanced perspective. We can attract more of it by focusing on what we want to expand. This can help us create a more fulfilling and joyous life.

As I examined my life and the areas where I had the most challenge, I almost always could trace it back to a negative thought or a subconscious program playing out unbeknownst to me. Dr. Lipton explains, "There are two parts to the mind ~ the conscious mind, which has your identity, Spirit, and source attached with it – is creative. The conscious mind can see into the future, review the past, solve problems. The subconscious mind, the other mind, is more of a habit mind. That's when you learn how to do something, and when you learn how to do it, you don't have to think about it. It's automatic."

Mind Games

According to Dr. Lipton, 95% of our daily habits are from the subconscious. He explains it's like a tape recorder playing old programs repeatedly. Most were programmed into us before age seven and from other people. These programs generally differ from what we know to be accurate or what we want. Even more disturbing is that 70% of what is being replayed is self-limiting, disempowering, and self-sabotaging. Most of the programs we are playing limit our abilities and take away our power. Our subconscious is constantly competing with our conscious mind. So even if our conscious mind wants to step on stage to be a speaker or start a new business, our subconscious may have a program running in the background, not allowing it to happen.

Years ago, a business coach told me I was 100% responsible for all the circumstances in my life—good, bad, and ugly. I was furious! I didn't sleep for a week wrestling with such an atrocious thought. I prayed and prayed that week. Because IF that were true — that I and others were 100% responsible for their lives—what about the bad things that happened to people?

Job loss. Rape. Cancer/illness. Car accidents — just to name a few!

There was no way I could comprehend that a person was responsible for such random acts of awfulness to themselves. I was awakened in the middle of the night as I wrestled with this. God and my Spirit team were showing me in a vision that yes, indeed, it's true. I am 100% responsible for what is happening in my life. However, there's more to it than meets the eye.

I was shown a computer with a simple program running. This represented my conscious mind. It was what I focused on and what I wanted to create each day. Glitches were happening, though. It kept closing unexpectedly. I would get the dreaded rotating circle of death where the computer froze. I began to examine if other programs were running that would affect this particular one. There seemed to be hundreds of other programs running — some I knew about, and I could easily see where they were open on the dashboard. But it took a computer expert to know where to find the other programs that were constantly running in the background. I could hear them running and yet had trouble locating them in order to disable them. This, of course, is a very simplified way of examining the programs that run us.

Even after seeing this detailed vision of how old programs run our lives, creating glitches in what we want to create, I still had trouble accepting that someone would agree to the awful things that happen in our lives. And, so, the lessons continued for me.

I was shown that my conscious vision of what I want to create is only a tiny part of the plan. As I mentioned, my subconscious was running the daily show, even though I attempted to create something completely different. It was as if I was playing tug-of-war with myself all day long. It was exhausting, and something needed to shift and shift FAST! Not only did my subconscious hold other people's programs (parents, siblings, etc.) that were installed onto my hard drive (a.k.a. ME) at an early age that was fighting with what I wanted to create, but it also held things we brought in with us from the Spirit world that we wanted to work on. All were pre-approved and pre-ordained. At the time, we agreed. Those are probably the challenging circumstances we said OK to, like an unexpected illness, the death of a child, or an accident.

Other allowances that followed us are past issues to be held in our subconscious for healing. Whether you believe in past lives or not, humor me momentarily. Let's say you had a past life (or several) where you starved to death. I do not doubt that it is now programmed into your subconscious to never starve to death again. However, now in this life, I suspect that no matter what you do to release weight, your

Mind Games

body is fighting you because it "just might" need the extra weight in case there isn't food.

Another example is a person who is an incredible healer and intuitive. Every time he steps out, though, he self-sabotages himself to stop his success. After pinpointing several past lives where when he did step out with incredibly gifted abilities, he was killed on the spot—guillotine, burned at the stake, and hung. No wonder he hesitated to speak his truth and step into his greatness! His soul remembers.

The mind is a powerful tool. It has even been described as a superpower; however, when not under your control, it can turn on you. If you constantly worry, overthink, or feel scattered, you're likely dealing with a "monkey mind."

A monkey mind is a term used to describe how our thoughts can race around and jump from topic to topic, much like a monkey swinging from tree to tree. The good news is that there are many ways to tame your monkey mind and find inner peace. Here are some of the best practices to help you gain control:

> **1. Meditation:** Meditation is one of the most powerful practices to calm a monkey mind. It helps you focus on the present moment and trains your mind to be more still and focused. You can start with a few minutes daily and gradually increase your practice as you feel comfortable.
> **2. Mindfulness:** Mindfulness is being fully present and aware of your thoughts, emotions, and surroundings. It can help you observe your monkey mind without getting caught up in its antics. You can practice mindfulness by taking a few deep breaths, paying attention to your senses, and focusing on the present moment.
> **3. Journaling:** Journaling is a powerful tool to help you process your thoughts and emotions. It can help you identify patterns in your

thinking and better understand yourself. You can try free-writing for a few minutes daily or use prompts to guide your journaling practice.

4. Physical activity: Physical activity is a great way to burn off excess energy and calm your mind. You don't have to do anything strenuous; even a short walk or gentle stretching can help you feel more grounded and centered.

5. Gratitude: Gratitude is a powerful practice to shift your focus from what's going wrong to what's going right. It can help you feel more positive and content, which can help calm your monkey mind. Try keeping a gratitude journal.

A monkey mind can be frustrating and overwhelming, and controlling it is not impossible. By incorporating these practices into your daily routine, you can find greater peace and clarity in your mind. Remember to be patient and gentle with yourself as you tame your monkey mind.

Many of us incarnated now are experiencing this push to be our best, yet our feet are often dug in the sand, not allowing us to move forward.

How do we program ourselves to receive positive thoughts and release the negative?

How do you create your ideal life when your body says NO?

How do you step out when your subconscious thinks you will get killed?

Making a true and lasting shift will take work from many angles and levels. The steps I have on repeat for myself are the following:

1. Clear my energy, auras, and chakras.
2. Reset my conscious negative thinking in the NOW moment.

Do the end of chapter RAIN meditation and other guided meditations.
3. Reset my subconscious thinking programming of the conscious mind. Get clear on what it is I want. Write affirmations in the present tense. Look through the list of affirmations at the end of this chapter. Rewrite for yourself, record, and listen to it each evening as you fall asleep.
4. Do the deep work of diving into your subconscious to reprogram it at the soul level. See Chapters 9 and 10 for a deeper dive.

I have a couple of quick tricks that I use almost daily. Instead of saying, "I never have enough time." I say, "I have plenty of time to get everything I need to be done." As soon as I say that second sentence above, my body calms into immediate peace. Another statement I often say to myself is, "Everything is always working out fantastic for me!" I say this when things are going well and especially when things aren't going as planned. Regardless, I'm telling God I trust that even though things may not look like I want now, I am trusting the process.

Now It's Your Turn!

Scan the QR Code below to hear Lara guide you through a deep light language meditation to reset the monkey mind. Have a pen and paper ready to journal your thoughts.

Scan me

Mind Games Meditations
Step 1:

I invite you to go through the RAIN process to shift your negative thoughts to a more positive, loving, and supporting experience. This can be done anytime, anywhere.

Unplug for a moment. Quiet yourself and observe.

R=Recognize what you are thinking that is causing your distress

A=Accept it (what we resist persists)

I= Investigate it — why am I thinking this? Do I want to continue to believe this?

N=Non-judgmental analysis of your thoughts — choose to "keep it" or let it go and change the channel of thought.

Whenever you are feeling overwhelmed with emotions or thoughts, remember RAIN. Imagine and feel the rain coming down on you and recognize what you're thinking and experiencing. Recognize, accept, investigate, and have a non-judgmental attitude toward it. Please continue to do this with each thought as it comes up for you.

Step 2: Go Deeper. Record for yourself the following or other ideal affirmations that resonate with you, and listen each evening as you drift off to sleep.

Anything in me/my energy field/subconscious in all time and space that does not align with the following statements MUST LEAVE NOW.

All other people's energies MUST LEAVE NOW and return to them.

It feels good to connect with my subconscious. I realize it's on my side. My programs run my life and my habits, and I am eager to connect to it and create a fantastic life and body.

My cells and nervous system are relaxing into optimum health, and they are being filled with the frequencies of love, joy, and calmness.

My DNA, Cells, Tissues, Organs, and Muscles are all in agreement and thrilled to hear these incredible instructions to create my ideal body.

My stem cells are now activated to return to their original healthy settings.

I have amazing vibrant health.

Everything is always working out fantastic for me.

I always manifest my dreams quickly and effortlessly.

I am creating love.

Money comes to me easily and effortlessly.

I'm more than enough.

I am a magnet for miracles.

I surrender any attachments to outcomes, and I allow the Universe to show me where to go and what to do.

I love myself in all ways, at all times.

I live in harmony with my body, and anything that doesn't align with that or my perfect health must leave NOW.

I trust the Universe is working on my behalf.

I am here to play, love, and enjoy life to its fullest.

I always have everything I NEED and more.

No weapon formed against ME, my home, business, or family, shall prosper.

Mind Games

I sleep deeply at night and wake up feeling refreshed each morning.

+ add any others that come to mind for yourself

6

Learning to Fly

*I'm learning to fly
But I ain't got wings
Coming down
Is the hardest thing*

~Tom Petty / Jeff Lynne

One beautiful evening overlooking the sun setting on the Gulf Coast, a friend and I sat on bar stools, chatting away. We were enjoying our dinner when suddenly I had to have ice cream! This was odd for me since I only had ice cream a couple of times a year. This energy to devour two scoops was so strong it knocked me off my stool! I caught my breath and looked around the room. Moments before, a lovely lady had slid in behind me at the bar. She was what would be labeled as obese and was ordering numerous items on the menu that were high in sugar. I suspected her blood sugars were off, and being as sensitive as I am, I immediately took on her imbalance. My back was to her, but that didn't matter. Our energy fields became entangled rather quickly due to proximity.

Whether you do this work for a living, struggle with energy sensitivity, or are curious about energy empaths, this chapter is for you.

You may shy away from crowds or desire to be alone. Your emotions may be overwhelming and ever-changing. These are all signs that you are picking up on others' energy and emotions. The more people awaken, the more empathetic they get. A new term you may also hear is—highly sensitive.

Numerous friends who do energy work healing like mine have quit their businesses due to their sensitivity. It can overwhelm our health, bodies, psyche, and emotions. I continually take breaks from providing client sessions to clear my body while learning new ways to take care of myself. I see, hear, know, and feel simultaneously, experiencing it on many layers. When I am present with a client or even a friend describing an event, my body receives the information in these several layers. I can see the story visually and intuitively; I may feel the pains or illness the person is experiencing in my own body at that very moment while hearing intuitively additional information regarding the circumstance. Not only is this the case with clients, but it also occurs in everyday conversation. Due to this high sensitivity, I am continually cautious about what I allow in my energy field.

Are you cursed with being too sensitive?

Have you been told that you were just too sensitive? Too emotional? Not enough and too much all at the same time?

When my ex-husband and I would take our kids to amusement parks, by early afternoon I felt awful and was curled up in a ball sitting on a curb. My body had proceeded to take on the emotions of people nearby, causing me to feel heavy, sick, and extremely tired. My husband would get frustrated at me because I had to leave the park to be alone. At the time, it was the only way I knew how to reset. I was overwhelmed by the crowds and didn't understand what was happening.

It would be years before I was made aware of an actual term for what I was experiencing—a highly sensitive energy empath. It was a relief to know I wasn't completely crazy!

You may feel the emotions and physical symptoms of others as if they were your own. If this rings true, you may be an "empath." Only a small percentage of the population experience this deep sensitivity, having the ability to feel and absorb the emotions surrounding them. There are hundreds of books and movies on the subject.

Highly sensitive people (HSPs) and Energy Empaths (EE) are individuals who are deeply in tune with their emotions and the emotions of others. They often have a strong connection to energy, and can pick up on the emotions and energies of those around them. While being an HSP or EE can be a gift, it can also come with its own challenges.

HSPs have a heightened sensitivity to the world around them. This includes being more aware of sensory information, such as light, sound, and touch, as well as emotional information, such as the moods and feelings of others. HSPs may also have a more vivid imagination and a deeper, vibrant life than others.

An EE is particularly sensitive to energy and can feel and perceive the energy of others and their environment. This includes being able to sense the emotions and moods of others, and the energetic vibrations of a space or location. EEs may also be able to perceive subtle changes in the energy around them, such as temperature or atmospheric pressure changes.

Being an empath and being empathetic are two different things. "Being empathetic is when your heart goes out to someone else; being an empath means you can feel another person's happiness or sadness in your own body," according to Judith Orloff, MD, a psychiatrist and author of "The Empath's Survival Guide." Another way to describe it is that an empath is like an emotional sponge—they absorb both the joys and the pains of the world around them, says Amanda Fialk, a licensed clinical social worker and an adjunct professor at Wurzweiler School of Social Work and Chief of Clinical Services at The Dorm, a treatment center in New York. "An empath does not simply understand someone else's pain; they sense and feel the emotions and feelings of their loved ones as part of their own experience."

In "Six Habits of Highly Empathic People," Roman Krznaric says, "But what is empathy? It's the ability to step into another person's shoes, aiming to understand their feelings and perspectives and to use that understanding to guide our actions. That makes it different from kindness or pity."

Are You An Empath?
- You need a lot of alone time.
- You feel others' emotions as your own.
- You are overwhelmed by crowds.
- You desire to help others.
- You are very sensitive to smells or materials.
- You are a great listener.
- You have to be alone to feel calm.
- You have a difficult time in romantic relationships.
- You have a hard time moving on from relationships.
- You notice little changes in people that others miss.
- You experience sympathetic nausea.

Once I realized what was happening, I learned to stop purposely taking on others' emotions. You may be there as well. You know you are sensitive and think it's your job to be the trash can for your community! You reason, "Aren't we made this way to help others?" No, we are not!

Yes, we were designed this way for a purpose. However, it's not to take on others' emotions, feelings, frustrations, and anger and pile them on top of our stuff. That's the martyred healer in us who suffers for others thinking it's our duty. It can even deceptively feed our ego to think, "Oh, poor me, I have no choice but to do this."

I used to think that being sensitive was a curse. I hated how I was and thought I had no say. I often hid in my house, saying I was sick, so I didn't have to go to parties that would overwhelm me. Now, I see what a colossal gift being an empath is! We are made this way to feel others' emotions, understand what they are going through, and support them.

You likely have a big heart that you could and would take on everyone's stuff to help them feel better. I often hear from clients, "But if I don't take on others' stuff, who will help them?" I do not know — maybe the next sucker who walks by and doesn't want to own their energy? Although I don't mean that as harshly as it sounds, I want to convey my point. We are all responsible for our emotions, thoughts, and circumstances. Suppose you continually take on others' stuff (even to your demise). In that case, you are meddling in their business of being responsible and learning life lessons of handling their energy, feelings, emotions, etc. You are prolonging their progress by taking on their energy, piling more discordance on yourself to process. Unfortunately, I had to learn this the hard way.

Being a highly sensitive or an energetic empath can profoundly affect your daily life. Here are some examples:

1. Overstimulation: sensory and emotional stimuli can easily overwhelm HSPs and energy empaths. This can lead to feeling overstimulated, anxious, or even physically ill.
2. Emotional Sensitivity: HSPs and energy empaths are more sensitive to the emotions of others, and may take on the emotions

of those around them. This can lead to feeling overwhelmed or drained and may make it difficult to set boundaries.

3. Sensitivity to Energy: Energy empaths may be more sensitive to the energetic vibrations of a space or location, and may feel uncomfortable or uneasy in specific environments. This can make it difficult to function in specific settings, such as crowded places or places with negative energy.

4. Empathy Fatigue: Constantly being attuned to the emotions and energy of others can be draining and may lead to empathy fatigue. This can result in feeling depleted, irritable, or disconnected.

5. Heightened Intuition: HSPs and energy empaths often have a strong intuition and may be able to sense things that others cannot. This can be a gift, but it may also be overwhelming or difficult to understand.

Basic Energy Empath Management

I'm a work in progress on this! I'm aware of my subconscious tendencies to think I still have to help everyone all the time, even to my demise. Meditations to release others (and my emotions) have become my daily practice. Empaths need to take special care of their inner lives and needs so as not to be overwhelmed by others, says Helena Rempala, a clinical psychologist at Ohio State University Wexner Medical Center. "A lot of them are good advice givers, very intuitive, and maintain deep friendships, but if you find yourself always giving but never receiving, feeling constantly sad or depressed, or are overwhelmed, it's time to ask for help," she says.

If you are a HSP or EE, considering the following could be game changers for you:

Meditation: (see page 200 for detailed info on meditation)
Affirmation: Make a choice and say often, "I choose detached empathy."

Take time alone: Review your calendar and ensure you are not over-scheduled.

Self-care practice: Make a list of the top 25 self-care practices and do at least one every day.

Grounding: Eating foods from the ground, exercise, yoga, and being in nature are all good options. Grounding and being in your body helps you stay in the moment and be more aware of where you end and where others begin.

SALT showers/baths: I load my hot bath up with two cups of Epsom salt and sprinkle several drops of lavender essential oil while soaking for a good 15 minutes.

The bottom line, be aware of your subconscious tendencies to believe you have to be a trash can for everyone else. You do not. But, it's your choice. Choose you! There's nothing wrong with empathizing with others in the moment. What we don't need to do any longer, though, is walk away from the conversation holding their emotional bag or taking their emotions home with us. If we do, our ego is fooling us into believing we can do that for them. In the meantime, I invite you to incorporate the meditation at the end of this Chapter into your daily practice to keep your energy clear of others so you can be your best.

Advanced Energy Empath Management

Although I knew I was consciously taking on others' emotions, I now see what an energy intrusion it is on both myself and them. In most instances, helping a butterfly out of the chrysalis will prevent it from ever flying, and the butterfly needs the struggle to strengthen its wings. Similarly, we do others a disservice by holding and processing their energies because it doesn't allow them to enhance their muscles to learn to fly. Often, another's energy and emotions enter through our sacral and solar plexus. So aside from the suggestions I've already mentioned, here are a couple of additional ideas for advanced energy management. Let's say you're in a group meeting, online or in person, feeling everyone's emotions and its overwhelming energy. Depending on the situation, I either detach my energy or put an invisible net over their energy field.

This allows me to lean in and connect with the person or the people talking without their energy leaking out and my picking it up. I'm not intruding. I'm not changing anything. I'm not even observing it. I don't need to know anything. It's holding their energy in for them. I'm doing the same for me so that neither one of us is enmeshing our energies, yet we are connecting.

Another energy hack is becoming present in our open chakras. Energy healer Jill Leigh has a simple visualization that we can use to reclaim our chakras. Imagine this with me: a ball of energy positioned in front of your spine, about two inches beneath your navel. Now imagine a vegetable steamer, wide open and pointing out in front of you on the ball's surface. So that's what your chakra looks like when it's excessively open. Take a pair of imaginary hands now and close the vegetable steamer petals down. You want just a tiny opening in the steamer. Do this a lot, over and over again. You will train your chakras to hold your emotions and not take on others. You won't miss a thing. I promise people will still tell you their stories and share their experiences. You won't hold them or carry them or watch them dance away while you hold all of their emotions. This was a game-changer for me. Your compassion emerges as a more elevated and neutral response.

Master Energy Empath Management

And so now for the fun level, the master level. If we continually tell ourselves and others (and I have been very guilty of this, too) how energy-sensitive we are, guess what? What we focus on expands!

> **Version 1:** I can't go to that party. There will be WAY too many people who want to talk to me, suck energy off of me and dump

their stuff on me. None of those people take care of their energy or their emotions. They are angry and cranky. They make me feel awful because I'm so sensitive. My body feels all their stuff. I can't eat anything there anyway because it's all processed crap. I eat only organic, gluten-free, vegan, keto, blah blah blah. I bet they will even use a microwave; those electromagnetic fields will get in the food, and I'll feel even worse. I'm "highly sensitive," and the music will overwhelm me. And, although I can handle holding everyone's unprocessed emotions, I don't want to put myself in a position where I have to tell them NO. They need help, and I'm here to help people. As an energy empath, I immediately feel all their pain and wild emotions as they tell me their stories. As a highly sensitive, energy-empathic sponge, it's too much because they won't deal with their stuff, so I have to do it for them.

Version 2: I can't wait to attend that event with my dear friend. I'll ensure I get plenty of rest before I go so I'm at my best. Yes, they eat differently than I do. I love being with them and honoring them where they are. I do not HAVE to do anything. I choose to stand in my power and my energy field. I am focused on BEING love and light. I can be IN the world and not OF it. I allow people to be who they are, without my believing they need to be or have something different or that I should change them. It's none of my business. No matter what food is served, I can bless it to change its vibration to align with my body. I have complete power over my own body and its energy.

I have experimented with both of these above versions. Which one makes me feel better? The second one, for sure. Words are energy, and words are spells. If we continue saying, I'm so sensitive, I'm an energy sponge. I feel everyone's everything, then that's exactly what will happen.

We all know that what we focus on expands. If we are focusing on taking on others' energy, that is what is so. Spiritual Mentor Alan Waugh writes, "What you are doing here is creating a self-fulfilling prophecy with your words and behavior. You create with your words and beliefs the invitation to the prevailing negative thought forms that you are willing (yes, willing) to absorb them. In the same way, when you say "I can't," you reinforce in your subconscious that you are willing and ready to fail. The energy of a victim, martyr, or sponge is weak or compromised, and affirms you are willing at some level to accept a foreign body into your energy field. If you choose words that enforce power, protection, and positivity, that is what you will attract."

And lastly, if you are still bothered by your energy sensitivity or anything else that you seemingly can't control, there is a way to reprogram your template at the soul level. Kyron says, "If you have an inappropriate remembrance in this lifetime that is affecting your life, all you have to do is acknowledge it with your body AND say we do NOT wish to have that remembrance affecting us in this lifetime." If you are unfamiliar with or would like assistance, work with an experienced Akashic record reader.

We have entered this life with many gifts and remembrances of the past. Often what we are "remembering" though, we no longer need. Remember the example of your body remembering a recent past life when you starved to death? Although you are surrounded by an abundance of food in this life, your cells hold onto every morsel of food to prevent you from ever starving to death again. And when taking on others' energy, your body remembers this as a similar program. Your soul template is programmed to gain/hold weight and take on others' energy. It's not good or bad. It's just a program that is running deep within your soul template. And, in your Akash is where it can be reprogrammed! I have done this on myself, reprogramming various programs with HUGE SUCCESS!

And this is a game changer to rewrite our remembrances. And this is where it's even beyond the subconscious. It is the template, the blueprint, that is running the subconscious. We can filter or reprogram our Akashic Records that aren't serving our best interests. We have that power! This is owning our energy, and I invite you to welcome these new basic, advanced, and master tool levels to manage your energy sensitivity. Below is a meditation for an energy clearing you can do for yourself. Reprogramming your Akashic records is something we do in private sessions or with an experienced Akashic practitioner.

Now It's Your Turn!

Scan the QR Code below to hear Lara guide you through a deep light language meditation to clear your energy. Have a pen and paper ready to journal your thoughts.

Scan me

7

Time to Move On

It's time to move on, it's time to get going
What lies ahead, I have no way of knowing
But under my feet, baby, grass is growing
It's time to move on, time to get going

~Tom Petty

Friends and family members wonder why I move so much. Jokingly, they ask me if I'm running from the IRS. No, the IRS owes me, so I keep my address updated for them. Nor am I "running" from myself, my emotions, or my life. If I were, I wouldn't be writing this book, that's for sure. "Can't you just be happy in one spot?" many ask me. I could, but I'm not meant to stay in one place. In addition to all the moving, I travel quite a bit. Most of my trips are never talked about, filmed, or photographed for remembrance. And certainly not posted on social media.

Although there is a method to my madness, with important reasons for all my moving and traveling, I seldom go into detail. I prefer to avoid drawing attention to my unique, behind-the-scenes metaphysical work. For whatever reason, I'm being led to reveal this part of my life I've kept primarily secret until now. I suspect this will answer questions for many others who will be reading this, assisting them in their journey.

What I'm referring to is being a Portal Keeper. Land healer. Energy clearer of land and space. Whatever you label it, it is. Only recently was I given a name for this backstage energy work I was doing. We, humans, have to label everything, don't we? It's helpful to organize and give us validity that we're not cuckoo.

I travel often, and when my trips never seemed to turn out as anticipated, I began to get curious about what was happening. Call me crazy, roll your eyes, but there is no other explanation except for this intuitive information I've been given to explain what I do or why I do it!

Portal keeping is the practice of maintaining energetic portals on the land. Portals are areas where the Earth's energy is powerful, and they can be used for various purposes, such as meditation, healing, and spiritual connection. Portal keepers are responsible for maintaining and protecting these areas, ensuring they are clean and free of negative energy. A Portal Keeper travels (physically or remotely) to a location to either live, work, or visit to hold and clear energy. They may not even know their presence in that space is clearing stuck, sad, discordant energies or resetting ley lines and grids of invisible energy. Often people do this with deep intention, like me, speaking light language, blessings, and praying over the home, land, or entire cities. Others have yet to perceive that they signed up for this portal-keeping adventure!

To explain deeper what a Portal Keeper is, here are a few definitions of these unique terms to move forward in this chapter with a better understanding.

A portal can be defined as an opening or entrance — physically or metaphysically. A property gate or website landing page can act as portals in the material world. In the spiritual world, a portal refers to a person, place, land, space, or object that acts as a channel for spiritual beings or energy to travel to and from Earth. Isn't a vortex the same as a portal? Not necessarily.

According to Amanda Linette Meder, "A portal is an opening, gateway, or bridge to another world, and a vortex is a spiral or pull of energy, sometimes attached to locations or created by geomagnetic forces."[11] Much information regarding ley lines can be found online, as they are essential to understand in work as a Portal Keeper. Wikipedia[12] describes ley lines as straight alignments drawn between various historic structures and prominent landmarks. The idea was developed in early 20th-century Europe, with ley line believers arguing that these alignments were recognized by ancient societies that deliberately erected structures along them.

Author Jen (no last name), "Alfred Watkins was the amateur archeologist who came up with the idea of the spiritual ley lines map in 1921. Riding his horse in the English countryside one day, he had what he referred to as a 'flood of ancestral memory.' While looking out at the gorgeous green landscape, he had an astonishing revelation. He realized that a network of lines stood out to him like 'glowing wires all over the surface of the country.' The grid-like markings are energy grids. He noticed that they ran in perfectly straight paths, also intersecting at places he called terminal points.

The fascinating part is that these terminal points often had sites such as beacons, holy, sacred wells, ruins, mounds, and churches. Panning back, Watkins also noticed that ancient sites at various points worldwide all fell into a pattern. They followed the lines. By seeing this and writing about it, he started a lot of controversies. He also set a thought process around the ley lines and supernatural and spiritual beliefs in motion. Further, they supposedly carry with them rivers of 'supernatural energy.' At the intersection point of these lines are said to be sections of concentrated energy, which specific individuals can tap into."[13]

Ley lines are invisible supernatural geographical lines that intersect throughout the world. Unlike latitude and longitude, they will not appear on a map, as they are lines of energy. The intersecting points create vortexes or spirals of energy, similar to chakras. Energy sensitives, like myself, can see or feel them. I especially notice the lines if they are disconnected or filled with dark energy. Other times, I sense superpower electricity running through them. Like a blood vessel in a person's body, a ley line carries immense power. Many believe potent energy centers can heal and align those interacting with them.

While most emit positive or neutral energy, some ley lines become disconnected or negatively affect the nearby inhabitants. This imbalance could be for various reasons, including:

- Geological stress or disturbances (e.g., fault lines)
- Collective negative thought patterns of the people along the line
- Disharmonious electronic radiations from underground streams or artificial radiation (Wi-Fi, microwaves, electricity)

It's the same as if a house's energy is off; if a ley line is disconnected, people or animals who live or walk over it may feel off balance — physically, spiritually, or energetically. Additionally, these circumstances may create episodes of the following among area residents:

- Confusion
- Feeling stuck
- Thick, muddy air
- Declining health
- Businesses not succeeding

- Unsettled, disgruntled employees
- Sudden unexplained illness or death
- Floods, fires, broken appliances or mirrors
- Excessive divorces, suicides, or traffic accidents
- Feeling like someone is watching you OR just an uncomfortable feeling
- Arguing among area citizens — especially at the local government level

Lightworkers are being called to serve as Portal Keepers and land healers to help restore balance and harmony to the Earth. By connecting with the energy of the Earth and working to heal the land, lightworkers can help create a better future for all.

To reestablish harmony, Portal Keepers are often led intuitively to these areas to reset the grids, vortexes, and lines. And I am no exception. Often without even realizing it, I am led to a place to do this unique energy work. At first, I thought I had a travel bug! An insatiable desire for an adventure to a specific place would overtake me until I finally went. Good thing I love traveling and exploring new places!

In the past, I would spend a significant amount of time researching gluten-free restaurants, natural grocery stores, yoga, hiking, and spas. All my favorite places! And what did I do when I got to my designated location? Nothing other than driving around! I barely had enough strength to get food, sightsee, or hike. I make plans, and God laughs. Or at least that's how it feels way too often. Regardless of my scheduled plans or hotels, if something felt off when I arrived, or I was led elsewhere, off I would go elsewhere' I'm usually led to go somewhere different, which involves driving in large circles while praying, clearing, and processing energy for people, homes, and land.

People ask me all the time, can't you say NO? Sure, and I will feel miserable because it's going against everything in my soul's essence. Somewhere along the line, I signed up for this job and am wired for it. There are many days that it's no big deal. At some level, I love seeing new sights while exploring the local scene. The processing of energy can be paralyzing, depending on what is going on in the city.

Some cities feel oppressed or depressed. Others, like college towns, feel lively with young, vibrant energy. Many cities embody sex-crazy party central, taking on the Spring Breakers' energy, while others feel flat-out dark and angry. Depending on the history of the land, death and destruction may be embedded into the dirt. The air may feel thick—physically and spiritually, or the opposite, light, airy, and breathable. Every single city is different.

When I visit larger cities—-such as New York City, Los Angeles, Miami, or Chicago—my body freezes in initial overwhelm and sometimes even physical illness. I feel like a human trash can processing these intense, overpowering energies, often suddenly ill with a cold, fever, or vomiting. When that happens, I rest in my hotel room for a day or two before I can venture out again. That extreme reaction was standard at the beginning of this travel work years ago. As my energy field has continued to gain strength' I've been able to manage the incoming vibrations much easier.

An upcoming travel trip usually begins with a nudge, "You should visit XXX." Then the nudge becomes more apparent: "Don't you want to go to XXX? There are people there you should meet." I'd much rather stay home in my comfy flannel jammies and do work remotely. Regardless, I begin being pulled (physically and emotionally) in a specific direction. And I know it will only stop once I investigate further. I am lured to a place one day, one step at a time. And, off I go.

They, as in my guides/angels/Creator/higher self/intuitiveness, go slowly with me. When they told me I was moving to Northern California two years ago, I told them to F-off. I'm not leaving Sarasota, my youngest son, friends, or the white powdery beach! And certainly not that far, and not California. Even in March, when traveling, I was adamant that I would not move to the Golden State. Well, we know how that went. Three months later, all my belongings I could fit were on a truck headed west. And, here I sit in Northern California on Thanksgiving Day alone, writing this book 3000+ miles away from my family and friends.

I planned a couple of weekends to write this book in Napa and Sonoma Valley recently. Uninterrupted time, except for a couple of winery visits, to focus on time with my computer. There was no writing either weekend. The first weekend was spent driving in circles (which is very common) to reset the ley lines and grids. Often a circle as large as hundreds of miles. During drive time, I speak in light language to send healing codes out to Mother Earth.

The following weekend was similar, except the deeper into the land I went, the sicker I became. I was in bed relatively early each night and woke up more ill. I struggled to eat, and finally, sad, frustrated, and lonely, I schlepped my bags back home with no other writing. I had planned to write, whereas the Divine planned to heal the land. Again, I make plans, and God laughs.

With each trip, I surrender more and more of my agenda. My ego and I were the only ones who turned that recent trip into a disaster because I didn't get done what I thought I should have. Isn't that just like us? Work, work, work. Instead of just being.

When I was married and raising my two boys, family responsibilities took precedence over my driving in circles to heal the land. My energy-clearing process at the time looked quite different than today.

Being a portal keeper doesn't come with a paycheck or a pat on the back. It takes its toll on me physically, emotionally, and spiritually. It's incredibly lonely and often debilitating. It costs me a lot of money, sleep, and friends, and it is almost always more work than play.

I get discouraged often and wonder when I will ever get to live my life. When will I ever feel normal with a successful business and husband? I begin to question and lose trust in God, My Creator. When I lose my connection with God, I lose my compass.

In July 2019, family friends, the Zildjian's, chose to celebrate the 75th birthday of their matriarch, Janet, in beautiful Umbria, Italy, next to Tuscany. I and a few others were invited to stay well in advance in the large home they had rented, Villa Fontanicchio. I said no rather quickly, rattling off my long list of excuses — including my business wasn't doing great and I had promised my son, who was getting married that year, money for his wedding. Although Italy was #1 on my bucket list of adventures, I let it go. Time flew by, and soon, my son's wedding was behind me. Mentally, the pressure was off, and my desire to go to Italy with these family friends grew. Before I knew it, I was on a plane for Rome, dreaming of pizza, red wine, cappuccinos, and fresh gelato!

Although this was a fantastic vacation overall, none of us realized what we were walking into. I was only a day into the trip before understanding the higher purpose. Whereas most people on vacation, especially in Italy, enjoy going to castles, cathedrals, the Colosseum, and other historic sites, I, on the other hand, tend to run in the other direction. When a site is listed as a historic site or museum, I will immediately get a visceral response to what energy is there. Often these places are protected because some battle occurred there or a burial ground sits upon them. I'm not there to have an enjoyable experience, like most. I rarely go to these locations because I almost always get sick by the end of the tour, processing energy.

And, as fate would have it, I was drawn to various sites even though I had no intention of going. My time in Rome was spent walking in circles around the Colosseum, praying in light language to clear the energy of the land and buildings. See Chapter 7 on portal keeping and land clearing.

As you probably already know, the Colosseum is famous for its magnificent stadium structure and the brutal history unfolding within its confines. During the Roman Empire, the Colosseum allowed more than 50,000 people at a time to enjoy its finest human bloodsport spectacles of gladiator fights, public executions, and animal hunts. I could hear the screams of the hurt and dying with every step. I could feel the death energy. I could see the ego battles intuitively playing out on a field of blood. I didn't set foot inside the Colosseum, and there was no need to make myself feel even worse than I already did.

With the Colosseum energy transmutation in my rearview mirror, I was thrilled to arrive in Tuscany at a beautiful property with a group of amazing souls. It was a breath of fresh air — for a few minutes, anyway!

Unbeknownst to me, no energy clearing I had ever done in the past compared to what was coming next. As I connected with the Zildjian's other friends who were visiting, the importance of this soul group reunion at this particular location began to unfold. The big story of that week isn't mine to tell, nor will I even try.

Energetically, the house felt like a hug. Although spirits walked around the house and property, their benevolent nature was more reassuring than scary. What was disconcerting, though, was a large lake off in the distance over the hill and on the other side of where the grapes and olives were growing. From the safety of our rental house, I would intuitively see people drowning while silent screams would echo in the water. A blood bath lay nearby imprinted on the land, as well.

Time to Move On

We soon learned this area was home to the famous Battle of Lake Trasimeno under Hannibal, who ambushed a Roman army. By the time the battle was over, 15,000 Romans lay dead, 5,000 had been captured; some 10,000 escaped into the hills. The lake turned to blood-red for a time as well.

My role in clearing disharmonious land sites always begins with asking Spirit what is happening and what the land needs. If a land area is crying out for help, usually there is some imprint of a battle, death, destruction, suicide, or a list of other things I look for. Over the years, I've made up my own checklist of things to look for. Once I know what's happening, the work begins. Always following Spirit's lead, I go in the order requested for what is best for that spot. It often includes talking to the deceased souls stuck where they passed, while assisting them into the light. After they have been escorted by their angels to the other side, safely basking in love and light, I ask that the land be filled with nothing but the highest vibration possible of love, joy, peace, and gratitude. Anything less in vibration, I ask that it be sent back to Spirit to be transmuted.

By the end of the week, with everyone's help in various ways, we felt like we had cleared the lake of its dark, harsh death and destruction energy. I had left on my way to another location for a few days before returning to the States. A 12-hour thunderstorm directly over the Villa came through, offering a further clearing ritual, ending in a rainbow with a cross of clouds etched in the sky. Our work was complete for that one small area in Italy.

If anything ever changed for residents near Lake Trasimeno, we will never know on this side of Heaven. What matters is our soul group got together (for whatever reasons in the beginning) to assist in balancing out the disharmonious energies that were prevailing. I also may never know exactly what I do or why I do it, and it doesn't matter. All I can say is my soul longs for travel and tells me where to go. Even on specific dates, I need to be in certain places.

This work is essential and challenging. Even if I can't see the benefits now, it's helping do something to heal the land or raise the vibration of the people who live there. I wouldn't wish this work on anyone. It's not something to take lightly. Trust me, I'm not laughing when I'm driving over a spot where a massive massacre took place. I can feel, see, know, and hear what went on in an instant — whether it was 5 minutes or 500 years ago. The land holds the energy and memories of the past, just like walls do in a house.

This work is unique for all who do it. This is a soul agreement I made long before I incarnated. Many of the men and women who are nomad travelers right now are portal keepers. Thousands have said yes to this calling for their life, including myself.

When I moved to Florida for the first time, I knew one person. I was making a big move after my marriage ended in Indiana, and was eager to establish a residency near the beach for what I thought would be for years. As I've said before, I make plans and God laughs! A year before my move to the West Coast, I was shown a man who was to take my place as the portal keeper in the Sarasota area. We all have some free will, and he and his family chose another assignment. I bought a house while attempting to settle in. My time in Sarasota was delayed another year. Although completely unpacked I felt quite unsettled. And, then, suddenly, I was released. It was a familiar, awkward push out of the city. Close friends and family members became distant. Everything feels difficult. Traffic, life. Even getting out of bed. Things stop working. I began to feel like a potted plant stuffed in a pot that couldn't grow anymore. My leaves were wilting while I stayed stuck in dry dirt.

When I hang my last photo and feel settled in my new home, I know

Time to Move On

it's time to go again. The wind picks me up and carries me to my next destination. I could fight it, and God knows I've tried. In the recent move from Florida to Northern California, I went kicking and screaming. 3000+ miles by myself. It was gut-wrenching and difficult for me to leave my family and friends in Florida. There was nothing written on paper that made this a good idea. I knew only one family where I was moving. Yet, my heart and soul said GO. I know the drill as I've done this enough times by now. Eleven moves in ten years and planning a twelfth now. A couple of months ago, I relocated to Southern California and now only a few months in, I know my time has come to a close.

I suspect I will be a portal keeper for my entire life; however, I can sense it shifting to a lighter responsibility, allowing for more joy and a fulfilling life for me moving forward. At the same time, others are stepping into their new role as portal keepers. Interestingly enough, I returned to Florida recently to visit where I had just moved from. I met a man who told me he and his wife, plus one other gal, had just moved from the area I moved to in California. What are the chances that I met this man? I felt God was showing me that we had all switched places to keep holding the energy and supporting each other in healing the land. What a blessing!

Now It's Your Turn!

Scan the QR Code below to hear Lara guide you through a deep light language meditation to heal the land. Have a pen and paper ready to journal your thoughts.

Scan me

8

Our House

> Our house is a very, very, very fine house
> With two cats in the yard
> Life used to be so hard
> Now everything is easy 'cause of you
>
> **~Crosby, Stills, Nash & Young**

When my children were school-age, complaining of tough days, not sleeping, or being frustrated, I would play their bedroom radios while they were at school on either a Christian or a classical music station. Time and again, I would do this without them knowing, while witnessing a shift in their mood. Within minutes of the kids going to their room, their cloud of sadness or frustration would be lifted. They would be laughing and eager to take part in family activities. Their rooms would get cleared of heavy, dense energy, and they would feel better. It would be years before I figured out what the music had done. They never knew either— until this book came out!

One afternoon, my friend Emma and I had our weekly private Bible study at my house. Although we attended different churches, I felt aligned with her deep love for God. We connected on a level that bypassed the doctrine of church walls. I had been telling her about fighting with my husband, seeing shadows in my house, and feeling fear run through my body. I had never heard of intuition, resonance, or vibration at this point in my life, and I certainly had never heard of energy clearing or house clearing. All I knew was that something in my house was frightening me and causing havoc. She and I walked into every room, praying in the name of Jesus. Emma would get intuitive hits on what was happening, and speaking in tongues often flowed through her. I don't believe either of us knew what we were doing, but we allowed ourselves to be guided by the Spirit of God to clear the darker energies in the house.

I remember vividly Emma standing in my son's room with her hand on the walls. She felt a dark presence in the wood beam beneath the paint and plaster. I also began to feel an unexplained heaviness, anger, and darkness filling the room. This room was my oldest son's bedroom, and he had recently asked me if he could switch rooms with my office. Very quickly after we prayed, we felt the Spirit of God clear the heavy dark energy from the room and the wood beam. Emma received the information that a workman on the house had gotten in a fight with a family member the day he was framing that room. He had opened himself up to dark energy with anger flowing into my house's foundation.

Hanging in my office was an art piece of a little Indian girl I had been gifted as a child. To all appearances, it was beautiful. However, when feeling into the photo, it felt creepy and possessed. That day Emma and I were house clearing, and we felt led to remove the artwork from my house and destroy it into hundreds of pieces to be sent away in the trash. Normally, now I do not destroy art, but in fact clear it just as any room.

These were a couple of examples of what Emma and I cleared that day in my home. I was in awe of the immediate energy shift and her blessed gift.

We had recently built this home in a new development in a suburb of Indianapolis, Indiana. It would be years later before I would fully understand the enormity of what I was just taught. The small neighborhood was wrought with divorces, death, gossiping, backstabbing, and illnesses. As I've continued my deep dive into the home and land clearing, I can easily see how the land we had unearthed for our beautiful homes was the sacred ground upon which many indigenous native deaths and sacrifices occurred. Even if it was hundreds or thousands of years ago, the land still holds the energy and memories of what happened there.

In Chapter 7, Time to Move On, I discuss portal keeping and land healing in detail. Land and home clearing go hand in hand. Generally, if after the home and people are cleared, there is still instability— it's an energy in the land. The land a home or business sits on should always be considered when a clearing occurs.

Have you ever walked into a room and something felt off? Or wondered what stories its walls would reveal? It could tell of joyous celebrations, comforting moments, and peaceful times. Happy memories of homemade ice cream with Grandma or children playing. Or it could reveal the chaos and turmoil that has taken place within its walls—disruptive memories as well, such as constant arguing between spouses or gossiping guests.

Negative or disruptive energies can come from various sources, including our emotions, the people and events in space, and even the land underneath a structure. Often though, the energy is from an outside intrusion of some sort. Aside from the occasional ghost or displaced spirit, there are disturbed nature energies, infected objects, open electronic portals, and trauma energies. Black magic, vows, and soul contracts can also affect the house's energy.

Realtors all over the country reach out to me often with help to clear a home that is not selling. In addition to the added stresses mentioned above, the current owner needs help letting go. Especially if they have lived in the home for a long time or if it was a family home, the owner could be having trouble letting it go, thus preventing the new potential owner from coming in. Even if the current homeowner says they want to sell, often subconsciously, they do not want to leave the familiar property. It was their home for years, providing safety and security. If they have yet to create a new place to move to, it is even harder to forge a new way forward. In that case, my prayer and intentions include a releasing technique. Another reason realtors need a house clearing expert is if there is a death or divorce in the house. These occurrences create an imprint in the house of death, anger, and grief that need special attention.

In my home, the main issues were from the land, the workman building the house, and an infected object. Fighting, illness, or even a death in the home or on the ground before the home was even built could affect your current health and mood. All walls, spaces, homes, and land retain living energy, like people and businesses. Everything, matter or non-matter, holds memories. We can't see memories, but our bodies, especially our homes, hold them.

Some discordant energies aren't even yours but affect you! It could be the power plant you live near, Wi-Fi, or other geopathic stresses. Electric discharges and other low-energy radiations cause havoc on our sensitive bodies. The home or business could be sitting on sacred land or a burial ground unbeknownst to you. Indians may have settled there long ago, leaving their imprint on the land. It could be a positive, encouraging signature or one of death and destruction.

Our House

Maybe you were previewing a home to purchase, and, although it looked perfect for you on paper, instead, you got a strange feeling. You couldn't explain it or put your finger on why. It was just knowing that you wanted to leave quickly. Thoughts, words, and emotions create bubbles of energy. This energy becomes embedded into our physical bodies and all our physical spaces, often staying stuck until they are cleared through prayer and focused intention.

Here are some signs that your house might need energy clearing:

- divorce OR remarriage
- declining health
- buying, selling, or building a new home or business
- feeling like someone is watching you OR just an uncomfortable feeling
- unexplained occurrences
- sudden unexplained illness or death
- arguing in home
- stressful living situation
- after a party/extra family living in the house
- experiencing stuck-ness or confusion
- business income decreasing or stagnating
- unsettled, disgruntled employees
- feeling drained
- not sleeping
- feeling overwhelmed

Like our bodies, our homes can become cluttered and stagnant with negative energy. It's essential to pay attention to the energy we bring into our homes and the energy our homes hold, as they can affect our mood, health, and overall well-being. To live a life of love and vibrancy, there must be flowing positive energy in your own body, homes, land, businesses, and even your car.

Home and space clearing removes this energy to create a more positive and harmonious environment. If you're experiencing any of the signs mentioned above, it could be a sign that your house needs energy clearing. Clearing the energy and blessing your home can restore balance and harmony to your living space, allowing you to feel energized, inspired, and supported. By removing the energy in your home, you can create a peaceful and harmonious space that supports your well-being and spiritual growth.

As the owner of your space and your body, you have the power to convert that energy. Energy cannot be created or destroyed; it can be transmuted into something lighter or moved to a new location.

- You may notice that numerous businesses move into a specific building or retail space, yet none seem to stay in business.
- A business is doing amazingly well financially until they decide to unearth some property next to them for an addition. All of a sudden, profits plummet and the staff is disgruntled.
- Families move into a beautiful home yet end up arguing or divorcing—one right after another. Neighbors jokingly say, "That house is cursed,"
- A new housing or business development is going in near where you live. Suddenly, the energies feel unstable near you, and staying focused is hard. You get flat tires, and family members and neighbors fight while weird occurrences happen daily.

Being in alignment and harmony with your home is more than just having a comfortable place to live. It is about creating an environment supporting physical, emotional, and energetic well-being. You will feel at peace and balanced. And, even during a stressful day, your home will support you with tranquility.

Energetically, being in alignment and harmony with your home means that the energy in your home is positive and flowing freely. When the energy in your home is balanced, you will feel more centered, grounded, and connected to the space around you.

Physically, aligning and harmonizing with your home means that your home reflects your style and preferences. It is a space that is comfortable, functional, and organized. When your home is physically in harmony with your needs and desires, you will feel more at ease and relaxed in your space.

Emotionally, being in alignment and harmony with your home means that your home is a place where you feel safe, secure, and supported. It is a space to be yourself, express your emotions, and connect with others. When your home is emotionally harmonious with your needs, you will feel more confident, empowered, and fulfilled daily.

Spiritually, being in alignment and harmony with your home means that your home is a space where you can connect with your inner self and higher power. It is a place where you can meditate, practice yoga, or engage in other spiritual practices. When your home is spiritually harmonious with your needs, you will feel more connected to your inner wisdom and guidance and experience a greater sense of purpose and meaning.

It's about creating a space that supports your physical, emotional, energetic, and spiritual well-being. By aligning your home with your needs and desires, you can create a sanctuary that nourishes your soul and helps you thrive in all areas of your life.

After I began working with clients to clear their energy, they would feel incredible. They would describe their demeanor as lighter, focused, and joy-filled, with an expanded intuition. However, within a couple of days of being back home, they would revert or not be able to integrate entirely the deep work we did at my office. I was shown that those who couldn't hold the frequency upgrades that occurred in our sessions often have homes that are not in harmony with their new vibration.

This aha moment of my client's homes not supporting them through their transformation reminded me immediately of my house years ago. I was walking around in fear and not sleeping well at night. Our homes are meant to be a sanctuary where we recharge, unwind, and feel safe. Unfortunately, all too often, I see homes wreaking havoc on lives. In personal sessions with clients, I always tune into their space to see if anything specific creates issues for them. If time allows, we will clear it right then. Otherwise, we schedule a specific house clearing at a later date. Families often hire me to do personal sessions with mom, dad, kids, and their house. I love working with entire families, supporting them in their shifts. Our kids and animals are uber-sensitive, feeling the daily energy changes even before they occur.

One simple way to begin improving the energy of our homes is to declutter and organize. Clutter can create stagnant energy, making it difficult to think clearly and feel peaceful. Take time to go through your belongings and remove anything that no longer serves you. Donate or sell items in good condition, and throw away anything damaged or unusable.

Another way to improve your home's energy is to bring in natural elements, such as plants, crystals, and essential oils. Plants can purify the air and add calming energy to your home, and crystals can absorb negative energy and promote positive energy. Essential oils can be used to uplift your mood and create a relaxing atmosphere.

As I mentioned, music and sound can play an integral role in clearing energy, including music, crystal bowls, bells, and other sounds. Music has been used for centuries as a means of healing and purification.

Different types of music can have different effects on the human body and mind. For example, classical music has been shown to reduce stress and promote relaxation, while upbeat music can increase energy and uplift mood.

Music has the power to shift our mood in an instant. Whether sad, anxious, or stressed, listening to music can lift our spirits, calm our nerves, and help us feel more positive and energized. At its core, music is a vibrational energy that travels through the air as sound waves. These sound waves can profoundly impact our bodies and minds, affecting our emotions, thoughts, and physical sensations. By listening to music that resonates with us, we can tap into this energy and allow it to shift our mood positively.

When clearing negative energy from a room, the key is to choose music that resonates with you and creates a positive atmosphere. Soft, calming music can help to create a peaceful and relaxed environment, while more energetic music can help to invigorate and energize the space. As in my children's case, although they weren't physically in the room to listen to it, the space received the high frequency to clear away any lurking lower vibrations, and they benefited later when they entered.

Crystal singing bowls are a musical instrument that produces a pure and clear sound when struck or played with a mallet. They are often used in sound healing practices to promote relaxation, balance, and harmony. Crystal bowls are believed to purify energy and clear negative vibrations from a space. The sound vibrations produced by the bowls can penetrate deep into the body and promote a sense of calm and well-being. They can also help to release blocked energy and promote emotional healing.

Bells have been used for centuries in many cultures around the world as a means of purifying and cleansing a space. The bells' sound vibrations dispel negative energy and promote positive energy flow. Many bells can be used for this purpose, including Tibetan singing bowls, wind chimes, and even handheld bells. When used with other sound healing practices, such as meditation or chanting, bells can be a powerful tool for clearing negative energy from a room.

In addition to music, crystal bowls, and bells, many other sounds can be used to clear negative energy from a room. These include:

- Nature sounds, such as running water or birdsong, which can create a calming and peaceful atmosphere.
- White noise, such as a fan or air purifier, can help drown out unwanted background noise and create a sense of calm.
- Mantras or affirmations can be repeated aloud or silently to promote positive energy and dispel negativity.

Finally, take time to cleanse and bless your home. You can do this by smudging with my favorite—dragon's blood incense or white sage, lighting candles, and praying. I personally channel light language and several other unique techniques in my client clearings. This can help dissolve negative energy and create a peaceful atmosphere. At the end of this chapter is a sample home-clearing ritual if you'd like to try it for yourself.

Also, on my website is my new Energy Clearing Kit, and be sure to download your FREE "If Your Walls Could Talk, What Would They Say?" eBook on DIY Home Clearing. By caring for our homes and being mindful of the energy we bring into them, we can create a space that supports our health and well-being, reflecting the positive energy we want to attract into our lives.

What to Expect After a House Clearing

House-clearing clients hire me for a variety of reasons. Mainly, they do not feel good in their space. Often they see shadows, hear odd sounds, or experience feelings of dread, even depression. There could be unexplained fighting in the house amongst family members, health could decline, or they feel stuck in life. Many clients have had ongoing plumbing issues, items being moved, and other unexplained occurrences.

To do a house or space clearing, all I need is the street address and if there's anything, in particular, you'd like me to focus on. The more specific and detailed my clients are with me, the faster the energy clears from the space. I've seen it take minutes or up to a month for a complete clearing on a larger property and business.

Patience and trust are needed at this time. I encourage you not to have any particular expectation other than KNOWING that the heavier, darker energies are being ushered out and lighter, happier, joyful energies are being escorted in replacement. It takes time to move a shovel full of dense energy set into motion with prayer and intention. Generally, if there are sounds or shadows, those cease immediately.

Depending on why you need a clearing, look for subtle clues to appear quietly in the background of your day.

Things to look for:

- Calmer household members/get along better
- People and space will be healthier, happier, feel lighter, and calmer
- More laughing. Less depression/sadness
- Items will not be falling off the walls; plumbing issues will cease
- New opportunities arise
- If the house is for sale, the house sells quickly and effortlessly
- Clarity returns
- Feel good in the space
- Sleep deeper

- Addictions will lighten

I am committed to clearing your space of the energy that holds you back and replacing that denser energy with a higher vibration. My ultimate goal for every house and space I bless is an energy that feels like a hug when you enter the room.

One Final Note

I believe house clearings and blessings are needed now more than ever. With the planetary shifts, millions of awakening souls are releasing dense energy into their homes. Additionally, lightworkers have become targets for darker energies, including AI, intergalactic dimensional beings, holograms, DJENs, demonic walk-ins, silvery intergalactic walkers, lizard-like reptilians, and even electrical implants into walls. I've also seen gargoyles numerous times in people's homes (also called Mothman). They look like giant flying monkeys from the Wizard of Oz. Nothing is off limits nowadays to the malevolent beings who desire to infiltrate people. They will stop at nothing to get pure-hearted light beings to quit their soul's work on the planet.

House clearings and blessings have existed for centuries and are deeply rooted in many cultures and spiritual traditions. These practices are designed to cleanse a home of negative energies, entities, or spirits and to invite positive energy and blessings into the space. The history of house clearings and blessings can be traced back to ancient cultures worldwide. In many indigenous cultures, the belief in spirits and energy is prevalent, and it is believed that these energies can affect the physical world. Shamans, priests, or other spiritual leaders in these cultures often perform rituals to cleanse and bless homes and protect the occupants from negative energies or spirits.

In the Western world, house clearings and blessings can be traced back to the Middle Ages. During this time, it was believed that evil entities could take over a person's home and cause harm to the inhabitants. As a result, people would often perform rituals to banish these entities and protect themselves from harm. The Catholic Church also played a significant role in this practice, with priests performing exorcisms and blessings on homes to protect the occupants from evil spirits. House clearings and blessings are still practiced in many cultures and spiritual traditions today. These practices are often used to cleanse a home of negative energy, promote positive energy, and protect the occupants from harm.

The benefits of house clearings and blessings are many. These practices can help cleanse the negative energy from a space, promote positive energy, and protect the occupants from harm. They can also help create a peaceful and harmonious environment, improving overall well-being and quality of life. The history of house clearings and blessings is long and varied, with roots in many cultures and spiritual traditions. These practices are still popular today. Whether you want to create a more peaceful and harmonious home or explore new spiritual practices, house clearings and blessings can be powerful tools for transformation and healing.

> Sally's husband had recently passed away in her house, and she was having trouble selling it. She contacted me before an upcoming open house asking for assistance clearing the energy, which sold in a week!
>
> A young mother, Amy, called me for help when her children began screaming as they were tucked into bed at night in their shared room. I intuitively saw her husband talking to an angry customer while sitting on the kids' room floor. The customer's energy had come through the telephone, planting itself in the children's room. As soon as I cleared the

angry energy from the room, the children began enjoying their room again.

Another client, Sara, reached out for help after several unusual occurrences in her house, including repeated flooding and wood pantry shelves falling to the ground. In addition to a friendly ghost in the house, some dark, heavy energies were in a few corners. And, although this homeowner didn't have any children, I "saw" several baby spirits playing in the backyard. Sara knew that the previous homeowner was an OB/GYN. I saw these many stillborn baby spirits had attached to this physician to come home to live at his home.

Eryn, CEO, said that after her business clearing, the short-term results were felt immediately, including a sense of a weight being lifted from her shoulders. The long-term results were numerous, as well. Employees who needed to exit left by themselves. The employees that stayed raised their awareness and vibration. Financially, the business was up $70,000 in 6 months compared to a year before. Eryn noted, "Lara has created an energy of healing and raised our vibration on a personal level, which translated into an elevated business and overall environment."

Now It's Your Turn!

To get started on your own house clearing, I recommend:

> Dragons Blood Incense Sticks
> Sacred Copal Incense Sticks
> 4-6 Black Tourmaline Crystals
> 1 Selenite (white stone) Crystal
> 1 Amethyst (violet stone) Crystal

Dragon's Blood has been prized as a grounding, powerful protector against negativity and lower vibrations.

Sacred Copal is a powerful healer and purifier, with the power to transmute negative energy.

Copal aids in physical, mental, and spiritual healing, and environmental clearing.

Black Tourmaline crystal is a powerful stone for protection against negative energy of all kinds, including psychic protection and EMF protection.

Selenite is an amplifier crystal and when used along with other crystals boosts their effectivity.

Amethyst is a stone of spiritual protection and purification, cleansing one's energy field of negative influences and attachments, and creating a resonant shield of spiritual light around the body. It acts as a barrier against lower energies, psychic attack, geopathic stress, and unhealthy environments.

Instructions:
Open all doors and windows, if possible.

"I call in the Creator of the Universe, the Creator of YOU. Your Higher Self, Your Angels, Jesus, Mother Mary, Archangel Michael, Archangel Metatron and your Spirit Team, who only want the highest and best for you.

I ask for Divine assistance today as I begin to clear this space. Please take away all lower, heavy energy and negativity that this area is holding, while filling it instead with your lighter, happier energies creating much joy.

Please bless me and my family as light flows into every corner of every room, through every door and space. Above, below, all around and in all time and space to allow us to feel your love that encompasses all. Thank you for all your support and help today." Amen.

Sit quietly in the room or house. Notice any impressions Spirit gives you or any information you need to know. There may not be any, but if so, make note of it. Next, begin to ask questions. Continue to write notes until you feel Spirit and your guides have told you all you need to know. Next, ASK them, "What is the best way to clear this land?" You will be guided the best way. Follow instructions per your team's guidance and make sure you thank them!

After burning either a dragon's blood or copal incense stick, place one of the four black tourmaline in each of the corners while placing a selenite and an amethyst anywhere in the room where you feel led. If you have extra black tourmaline, place one above both the front and back doors so that as people come/go their energy will be cleaned.

Repeat incense burning as needed. For myself, when I am clearing a house, I put my iPad in one room and my phone in another each playing my light language clearing meditations. I walk around saying my prayers while tuning in.

If you would like more specific guidance on home clearings, go to LaraJaye.com for online classes that include clearing checklists.

Scan the QR Code below to hear Lara guide you through a deep light language meditation to clear your house. Have a pen and paper ready to journal your thoughts.

9

Dancing With Your Shadows

It's hard to hear your words
When you're so afraid to speak them
Something's on your mind
But you're hiding it away

It breaks my heart
That you can't let go
You say you're fine
But girl I know

You've been dancing dancing dancing with your shadows

~Phillip Phillips

I stumbled upon shadow work without knowing what I was doing. As I leaned into my intuition, I was guided to my next step or whatever I needed to know. Often the downloads didn't make sense at the time; however, a day, month, or even years later, I see the puzzle design form perfectly. Although I've tried almost every healing modality available, the ones that made the most headway in my transformation were those given to me directly from Spirit. Those processes are what I am sharing in this book. Old souls on this planet need unique tools and techniques to assist them in letting go of what holds them back.

It usually starts with a heavy feeling in my body or just feeling out of balance. I've had enough good days to know how awesome I can feel on a high-vibe day, so when there is an issue I need to work through, I'm given an odd feeling that won't go away until I examine it. My morning prayers and meditations are when I slow down enough to hear what Spirit says. This is the time when I process any energy that feels heavy. And then, I began to call back and meet all the different aspects that make up the whole of me.

I begin by tuning into my body and asking what is going on. I keep my laptop or iPad close by and journal in the Notes section. Most of this book was written in my Notes section and transferred later to my Scrivener writing program for ease of editing. I close my eyes while typing nonstop, tuning into what my body wants to say to me. Usually, there is an area on my body that is pinging. It's a red siren sign for I WANT ATTENTION!

I don't normally plan what inner work I'll be doing that day. All I know is, whatever is screaming for attention, that is where I tune in. It could simply be stuck energy that needs to be moved. Or a psychic attack from someone else. It could be a soul fragment ready to return or a soul aspect ready for transformation. I am made aware of where I am out of alignment only when I slow down enough to hear the whispers of my body and soul.

For example, currently, my stomach is pinging me. I go deeper. I feel a punch in the stomach. This area is my power center, called the Solar Plexus. It's where our confidence and self-esteem show up. We also take in others' energy, or they can easily attach to us if we're not careful in this same area. I continue to focus on what it wants me to know.

I rule out...

- An attachment
- A cord
- A psychic attack

Intuitively, I'm being given the information that a personality aspect of me resides in this chakra that is not aligned with or in harmony with my greater personality. I dive even deeper.

I ask myself, "In what area is this aspect not in alignment?"

I hear "HEALTH."

I've had stomach issues for a while, so the information made perfect sense. I had been feeling as if my body was working against me. This particular aspect of myself exemplified the energy of working against me and was perpetuating ill health in my body. This aspect was the root cause of many of the issues. To transform this aspect of myself to be in harmony with my more aligned vision for my life, I isolate this aspect, handling it with love and care. It is on a mission to create ill health for me; the opposite of what I desire.

I ask the aspect to step forward. It's as if someone or part of my personality steps out of my body and turns to face me. Doing so helps me to isolate the aspect, see the energy of it, and what its true intentions are. In this case, I hear that the aspect is old and has been around for generations. I see parasites swimming around. They are not necessarily physical parasites (although they could be), or toxic people in my life. Just today, a nutritionist mentioned that deeper meaning of the autoimmune condition I have, Hashimoto's, is, "People being drained by parasites in their life." Well, if that isn't fitting!

This aspect of myself facing me looks like an older person with black goo all over them. Forlorn face, depressed, and large—although shrinking. It is feeding off fear and ancient energy. I'm being shown that their energy source (to feed the ill health) is no longer attached. This creates a situation for this aspect to make itself known to me—finally. However, it's asking me for a new energy source to feed it more illness. Too bad for it; I have other plans!

I ask Creator to speak to this aspect of myself, showing it my divine plan for me in this life. I wait in silence while this aspect of myself is being shown, almost like a movie playing out in front of us, the highest possibilities for me. After that is complete, I ask the aspect if what they represent is in alignment with my highest expression, and if not, are they willing to transform to help me to live out that life with perfect health and harmony? I get varied answers from different aspects for different purposes. Today, this aspect does not want to support me.

Aspects, although a part of you, can live in another time and space AND they can have separate vows, contracts, agreements and remembrances on them. The aspect I worked with on this particular morning had all that happening. This aspect is tied to another time and space where it has an agreement to carry out ill health.

This will be a bigger job than simply asking the aspect to live harmoniously with me. Going even deeper in time and space, I ask Creator to dissolve all vows, contracts, agreements and remembrances for anything that doesn't align with perfect health in all my cells across all time and space. I continue with Light Language energy for clearing and observe.

My stomach begins to rumble as I feel it is unhooking from my body and dissolving before me, almost melting but turning to pixie dust.

I ask questions to double-check that all is complete.

Is the aspect completely dissolved within my energy field and cleared throughout all time and space?

If yes, continue with gratitude.

If not, ask more questions about what else you need to do for it to dissolve completely.

This work is an example of integration of an aspect shadow personality. This could have gone several different ways. Often the aspect wants to transform and stay with you. If that is the case, do the same light language and allow it to integrate within yourself.

During a typical energy session, I'm working with parts of the client's soul that aren't necessarily in this time or space, yet they are connected. Soul fragments, shadow work, past life regressions, and soul aspects (or personality) integration are all vital parts of the transformative journey I embark on with my clients. Exploring the depths of the soul and its various dimensions allows us to address unresolved issues, release energetic blockages, and restore harmony. By delving into the realms beyond what is immediately perceivable, I assist individuals in uncovering hidden truths, healing deep wounds, and ultimately integrating fragmented aspects of their being. These profound techniques enable us to tap into the boundless potential of the soul, facilitating personal growth, self-discovery, and a profound sense of alignment with one's authentic essence.

Energy sessions are a sacred space where time and space converge, transcending conventional boundaries, to access the realms of the soul. In this holistic approach, the focus extends far beyond the limitations of our current existence, reaching into the vast expanses of spiritual realms and alternate lifetimes. By acknowledging that the soul's journey extends apart from a single lifetime, we can understand the complexities of our experiences and the interconnectedness of our existence.

As the term suggests, soul fragments are pieces of our essence that may have become fragmented due to past traumas or challenges. These fragmented aspects can hold energetic imprints that influence our present reality, causing emotional and energetic imbalances. By skillfully navigating these realms, I guide individuals through a process of integration, helping them reclaim lost fragments, heal wounds, and restore a sense of wholeness.

Shadow work, another crucial aspect of these sessions, involves delving into the depths of our subconscious mind and exploring the aspects of ourselves that we have suppressed or disowned. By bringing these shadows to light, we facilitate deep healing and promote self-acceptance, unlocking the dormant potential within.

Furthermore, past life regressions open doors to the vast tapestry of our soul's journey, allowing us to access memories and experiences from previous incarnations. Exploring past lives can provide profound insights into our present challenges and shed light on recurring patterns, offering opportunities for resolution, growth, and spiritual evolution.

Lastly, soul aspects or personality integration involves embracing and integrating various aspects of our multifaceted nature. We have different facets, archetypes, and personality traits contributing to our unique expression. By honoring and integrating these aspects, we can harmonize conflicting energies and cultivate greater self-awareness, authenticity, and empowerment.

In these transformative energy sessions, the boundaries of time and space blur, granting us access to the profound depths of the soul. Through soul fragments, shadow work, past life regressions, and soul aspect integration, I accompany my clients on a remarkable journey of self-discovery, healing, and integration. Together, we traverse the uncharted territories of the soul, unlocking hidden potentials and fostering deep alignment with their true essence.

During an initial clearing, we almost always call back soul fragments to the person. A soul fragment is a portion or part of an individual's soul that has separated or fragmented from the whole. This fragmentation can occur for various reasons, such as traumatic experiences, intense emotional events, or spiritual disconnection. The individual's soul may not be fully integrated or functioning optimally when a fragment occurs. The goal is to heal, reintegrate, or retrieve these fragmented parts to restore wholeness and well-being. I highly recommend working with a trusted, experienced energy practitioner to retrieve soul fragments. As the client integrates their newfound pieces after a retrieval, they will most likely desire to transform shadow personalities or aspects that could hold them back.

Soul Aspect Healing

As mentioned above, a soul aspect (or personality) refers to a specific facet or expression of an individual's soul, akin to a distinct personality or energy pattern within the larger soul. These aspects have unique qualities, experiences, and purposes, such as creativity, wisdom, compassion, or courage. They contribute to an individual's overall growth, learning, and soul journey, manifesting in different circumstances and times. And, although connected to you at all times, these aspects (possibilities hundreds) can exist in other times and spaces and have their own vows, agreements, and contracts.

The concept of healing a soul aspect is associated with spiritual beliefs, and involves addressing imbalances, wounds, or traumas that impact the soul or spiritual essence. This healing process delves into the deeper layers of one's being, exploring past life experiences, karmic patterns, soul contracts, and spiritual growth. Meditation, energy work, past life regression, or connecting with higher realms of consciousness are typically employed to heal a soul aspect. Guided by Spirit, individuals may invite a relevant soul aspect to make themselves known when struggling with a particular issue, allowing for its healing and integration.

While shadow work is a specific aspect of healing soul aspects, healing soul aspects can encompass a broader range of approaches and techniques to address spiritual and emotional healing. Shadow work specifically focuses on exploring and integrating the shadow aspects of oneself, whereas healing soul aspects may involve addressing other spiritual or energetic imbalances beyond the shadow.

Shadow Dancing

We tend to focus on our positive attributes and accomplishments when we think of ourselves. However, there is a side of ourselves that we tend to ignore: our shadow side. The shadow side refers to those aspects of ourselves that we repress, deny, or hide from the world. These can be negative emotions such as anger, jealousy, fear, or past traumas and repressed memories. We often ignore or reject the dark side of our personality because we see it as undesirable or unacceptable.

The famous psychologist Carl Jung first introduced the concept of shadow work. Jung believed acknowledging and integrating our shadow self is essential for personal growth and development. When we refuse to confront our shadows, it can cause inner turmoil, depression, and anxiety. If left unaddressed, we may experience negative emotions, self-doubt, and self-sabotage.

Shadow work involves acknowledging and embracing these aspects of ourselves and working to heal and integrate them. While shadow work can be difficult and uncomfortable, it is an integral part of our spiritual journey, as it allows us to release limiting beliefs and patterns and step into our power and authenticity. Healing your shadow self is essential for personal growth, spiritual development, and emotional healing. This process can be facilitated through various therapeutic techniques, inner reflection, journaling, meditation, or working with a trained professional.

While there may be overlaps in the concepts of healing a soul aspect and healing a shadow, they address different dimensions of an individual's inner journey. Healing a soul aspect tends to focus on the spiritual and transpersonal aspects of self, while healing a shadow is more centered on psychological and personal growth.

Monsters Under My Bed

At night time, I would jump into bed from afar. As an adult woman, it was very odd, even to me, that I seemed to have fear around what was under my bed. The fear continued for several months until I finally slowed down enough to ask questions. This happens when our soul screams to be heard, and we ignore it, as I did! Spirit had to get creative with me to get my attention.

Finally, in the daylight, I sat on my floor and looked under my bed. Nothing was there in the physical, as I had suspected. However, I could feel something was there. I closed my eyes and intuitively shined a light on the situation. I would sense black globs of energy. For each one, I would tune in deeper, understand its meaning and either integrate it into myself or return it to Spirit for transmutation. The monsters under my bed were Spirit's way of showing me my shadow parts, past lives, aspects, or even relationships that needed attention.

This work went on for months, with occasional nights off of the work.

I knew when I got in bed at night that if I sensed something under my bed, I wouldn't sleep until I acknowledged it.

In an effort to not have any more monsters under my bed, I became proactive in my daily soul aspect integration work during my morning meditation, as I describe in detail above. Clients also became fascinated with the more profound, deeper work. To process shadow aspects, I go into meditation and call forth the part related to whatever issue we are addressing for myself or the client.

Healthy Eating Resistor

During a coaching session with client Sarah, we called up an aspect of her resisting healthy eating. The energy was giant and jagged. It had a demon-like face in a pile of undigested poop! As I sent it love and light language, it shrank, melting into the ground.

Unloved & Unseen

In another session with Sarah, we called up the personality part of her that felt unloved, unseen, unheard, and untouched. This depressive energy was a giant. Her guides were showing me because it was so strong in her field that she continued to attract more circumstances that strengthened this aspect. As we sent it gratitude and love, it began to take a standard persona shape. It relaxed, and her world began to reflect the opposite of what it was attracting.

Protector

Client Roberta, met the part of her personality that is her protector. Her knight and bouncer. He was strong and masculine and took his job seriously, defending Roberta and keeping her safe from men. He was doing a bang-up job for Roberta keeping men, love, and community away from her; she was starving for love. After sending her Protector light language and love, we asked him to shift his responsibilities for

Roberta to that of a discerning protector, allowing in love and kind people.

Business Fail

When I was recently working with James, a recent past life was revealed as affecting his entrepreneurial success today. He had created several businesses, which all failed to produce a profit. He had died penniless and embarrassed. Coming into this life, he had the energy of failure throughout his entire body. He was beginning to feel like a failure again, preparing to close the doors of a new business when he and I uncovered this information. After clearing the past energy, he could pivot his business for a huge success.

Shadow work can be a little unsettling at first, but after you begin to understand the depth of your soul, you will find it fascinating as you quickly resolve hidden issues. At the end of the chapter, I will outline my process for integrating a shadow, and for now, you can begin these steps for yourself:

> **1. Self-awareness:** The first step in shadow work is to become aware of the parts of yourself that you tend to ignore or deny. Take some time to reflect on your negative emotions, past traumas, and fears. Start a journal where you can write down your thoughts and feelings.
> **2. Acceptance:** Once you have identified your shadow self, it is essential to accept it without judgment. Remember that everyone has a shadow side, a natural part of being human. Embrace your shadow and acknowledge it as a part of yourself.
> **3. Compassion:** Shadow work can be a complex and emotional process, so it is essential to approach it with self-compassion. Be gentle with yourself and allow yourself to feel your emotions without judgment.
> **4. Integration:** The ultimate goal of shadow work is to integrate your shadow self into your whole self. This involves acknowledging

and accepting your negative emotions and past traumas and working to heal and integrate them. Seek therapy or support from a trusted friend or mentor.

5. Practice: Shadow work is an ongoing process, so it is essential to practice it regularly. Reflect on your emotions and experiences, and be open to learning and growing.

Past Lives

Part of shadow work can involve examining past life issues that may have been carried over into this life. For several reasons, examining past lives can be crucial in specific spiritual and therapeutic frameworks. While the concept of past lives may not be universally accepted or supported by empirical evidence, those who believe in reincarnation or the continuity of the soul across lifetimes find value in exploring past life experiences. Here are a few reasons why examining past lives can be considered significant:

> **Understanding patterns and unresolved issues:** Past life exploration can provide insights into recurring patterns, behaviors, or emotional responses that are difficult to explain solely based on one's current life experiences. By uncovering past life memories, individuals may gain a deeper understanding of the root causes of specific challenges, fears, or traumas they face.
>
> **Healing unresolved traumas and wounds:** Past life regression or exploration techniques aim to address and heal unresolved traumas or wounds that may have originated in previous lifetimes. By bringing awareness to these experiences, individuals can work through associated emotions, release energetic imprints, and find closure or healing for persistent issues in their current life.
>
> **Spiritual growth and soul evolution:** For those who believe in the soul's spiritual evolution across lifetimes, exploring past lives can offer a broader perspective on the soul's journey. It can provide a

sense of continuity, purpose, and lessons learned throughout multiple incarnations, contributing to personal and spiritual growth.

Release of karmic patterns: Some belief systems suggest that karmic patterns, the consequences of past actions, can carry over from one life to another. By examining past lives, individuals may become aware of karmic debts or imbalances that need to be addressed and resolved in order to break free from repetitive cycles and move toward greater harmony and balance.

I didn't believe in past lives or other dimensional aspects for most of my adult life. Until I began to do this work for myself, did I realize the importance of exploring this buried energy affecting my everyday life. Bringing an open mind, discernment, and respect to exploring past lives is of utmost importance. Individuals have varying beliefs and interpretations regarding past life experiences, and the significance and impact of such exploration can vary from person to person. It's a personal journey that should be undertaken with respect for one's own beliefs and the guidance of qualified professionals or practitioners experienced in past life regression or exploration techniques.

My role with a client is acting as a midwife. I hold space, access intuitive information, and lead the birthing process. The work, though, is done in the inner psyche of the client. I can assist in moving stuck energy, allowing the client to have a head start in facilitating their own transformation.

Shadow work, past life regressions, soul aspect, and personality healing are vital to personal growth and development. By acknowledging and embracing these hidden sides to ourselves, we can heal and integrate all parts of ourselves, leading to a more fulfilling and authentic life. This work is a process that takes time and patience to integrate fully. Be gentle with yourself and trust the process.

Now It's Your Turn!

Scan the QR Code below to hear Lara guide you through a deep light language meditation to meet a shadow personality aspect. Have a pen and paper ready to journal your thoughts. We each have hundreds of shadow personalities inside of us that are waiting to be acknowledged and integrated. And when we're having trouble accomplishing something, it's generally because we are actually sabotaging ourselves. For this meditation, I have provided an example of you meeting your PROTECTOR that holds you back from stepping into your highest expression of yourself.

You can do this visualization as often as you like, substituting the PROTECTOR for other personality aspects to create alignment. For example, think about what challenges continually occur in your life.

Is your health a continual fight? Call upon the aspect of yourself that allows your health to deteriorate.

Do you struggle to lose weight? Then let's meet the shadow aspect of yourself that prevents you from reaching your goal.

Is finding meaningful work a challenge? Ask to meet the personality aspect that believes work should be hard and meaningless.

10

Just Be Held

Hold it all together
Everybody needs you strong
But life hits you out of nowhere
And barely leaves you holding on
And when you're tired of fighting
Chained by your control
There's freedom in surrender
Lay it down and let it go

So when you're on your knees and answers seem so far away
You're not alone, stop holding on and just be held
Your world's not falling apart, it's falling into place

I'm on the throne, stop holding on and just be held
Just be held, just be held
If your eyes are on the storm
You'll wonder if I love you still

~Casting Crowns

Yesterday, a friend told me my light was missing. I know it's there. Our lights are always there inside of us, waiting to be uncovered.

Today, mine feels hidden in a pile of black goo! This burden on me is weighing me down so much that on most days lately, I have very little to give. I get angry that things aren't going more smoothly for me. I have dedicated my life to helping others, yet some days I cannot help myself. It doesn't seem fair or make sense. And why, even though I do what I think is right, am I still not moving forward? And, the question is, based on what? I've learned that Source is more concerned with our soul growth than how many followers we have on Instagram or our bank account balance.

As I sit here in meditation this morning, I am steaming. Some super spiritual mentor I am! I woke up agitated, angry, frustrated, and resentful. Why? Because I still am not in this life where I desire to be. I've strived, tried, paid, pushed, pulled, and jumped up and down to no avail. On most days, I can go into prayer and meditation to release these frustrating feelings; however, they are not budging today. I am feeling even angrier while bubbling up from the depths of my Soul.

So here I am. This is my prayer and meditation time, and I'm steaming like a boiling pot. I didn't feel this way yesterday. What happened, I ask myself?

Let's back it up 12 hours, right before I went to bed — I received a text message from a friend who was agitated, angry, frustrated, and resentful. Sound familiar? He was very unhappy in his life and wanted things to be different. I do not doubt that those intense emotions attached themselves to me right before I fell asleep. I still have an open wound for them to connect to. Do I blame him for sending me bad juju? No, it's all on me. I am 100% responsible for everything in my life and energy field. Whether it's mine or not, if it's there, I am the one who needs to handle it. Here's what I would do differently, though.

Better boundaries. Wait to answer the phone or texts after 5 p.m.

Take the time to feel and clear myself before I go to bed.

I'm partly mad at myself for answering the text. I have good boundaries with clients, but a tad looser when it comes to friends. We live and learn with each circumstance. In the past, in my own emotional 911 emergencies, I would go down the never-ending rabbit hole. Beating myself up, emotionally in my mind. Asking myself, "What's wrong with me?"

Usually, when I begin to feel the way I describe above, I can go into meditation and prayer to clear those low-vibe emotions. Today, not so. Occasionally, my frequency gets zapped into a dark night that takes longer to climb out of. Because I haven't cleared this yet, it's still in my energy field, and I feel nauseous. The mind blows up my emotions like a balloon, ready to pop. I'm losing energy; my body is becoming weaker.

I'm not exempt from feeling this hell of the dark to appreciate the light. There isn't much that I haven't experienced. Aside from a miscarriage (that I'm aware of) or living on the street, I have been blessed with many other life experiences that have ripped the road out from under my feet while punching me in the stomach and dragging me in the dirt. With each one, I learn more lessons, surrender at an even deeper level, and let go more.

When I'm feeling this down, I call it a *dark night of the soul.* This term originates from the writings of the Christian mystic St. John of the Cross, but has also been adopted in a broader spiritual context. It refers to a profound and intense period of spiritual crisis, where an individual experiences a deep sense of spiritual desolation, existential questioning, and disconnection from a higher power or meaning. It is often characterized by emotions of emptiness, despair, and a loss of faith or purpose. The *dark night of the soul* is considered a transformative and purifying process, where the individual undergoes profound spiritual growth and purification, and ultimately emerges with a deeper understanding and connection to their spirituality.

It is often described as a necessary stage of purification, where one's ego and attachments are stripped away, leading to a deeper connection with the divine or the true self. During the *dark night of the soul*, individuals may experience a loss of meaning or purpose, feelings of isolation, and a profound longing for something beyond their current state. It can be a challenging and painful journey as individuals confront their deepest fears, unresolved issues, and the aspects of themselves that they may have been avoiding or suppressing.

The *dark night of the soul* is not necessarily a literal night or a fixed period, but can last for varying durations, ranging from weeks to years, depending on the individual. It is believed that those who emerge from this experience often gain greater clarity, inner strength, and a deeper connection to their spirituality or a sense of purpose in life.

I have had many dark nights that have lasted those varying timeframes and degrees. At this point, I know that there is light on the other side even when I'm in the darkness. Although this helps contextualize the inner pain until I surrender to it thoroughly, learning what to do for transformation. I process a dark night in several ways, depending on how it shows up.

Winter times in Indiana are bleak and dreary. It was a given that I would be a little more depressed when December arrived. After the spring ice and rain storms subsided, I usually would pop out of it, welcoming the sunshine. Over the years, though, even the summer sun couldn't break through the deep sadness that prevailed. Seventy-five degrees, breezy and sunny, didn't stand a chance to cheer me up as

I lay in bed, staring out the window, crying the entire day. Again, I asked myself, "What's wrong with me?"

What's wrong with me that I am so lonely?

What's wrong with me that my hair is falling out?

What's wrong with me that I'm so sad?

And what happens when you ask those defeating questions, you receive defeating answers. You are shown all the reasons something is wrong with you. It's a Universal Law to answer the question you are asking. Think about that question momentarily, "What's wrong with me?" Feel it in your body. How does it feel? Light and airy? I doubt it. Just as I'm writing this chapter, my body feels heavy. My chest (my heart chakra) is tight. Instead of asking myself, "What's wrong with me?" I shift the energy by asking myself a different set of questions, such as:

What's right about this situation?

What's right about me feeling lonely?

What's right about my health issues?

What's right about me being alone?

What's right about…

Or what's my next step…

Already writing these different words, I feel my energy lighten. My chest expands as I take a deep breath of happiness.

Another way I process *dark nights of the soul* is to tune into my body and ask questions while journaling to process deeper feelings. Although this takes effort and time, I often don't want to take it; but I always reap the benefits from leaning into the unseen blocks. I begin by tuning into my body and describing my feelings as I write. Below is a recent example.

I'm in a pressure cooker. It's hot. I'm angry. I am inflamed. My body feels inflamed. I'm looking for anything in this metal pressure cooker to ease the pain.

I've tried writing.

I've tried sugar.

I've tried screaming.

I've tried sleeping.

I've tried crying.

I've tried alcohol.

I've tried watching tv.

I've tried praying.

Nothing seems to work. My body hurts everywhere. I feel like there is a tube going down my central spine —right through my central nervous system, keeping me grounded and stuck in one place. I want out. I want to feel something different. I want to handle anything less painful than what I am right now. Then, I realized the pain moving through my body couldn't hurt me. I take a deep breath. I relax into my body.

I surrender to the moment of it.

I surrender to the pain.

I surrender to the anger.

I sit down in it.

I ask "it" what it wants me to know. It answers, "I just want to be acknowledged. Please don't ignore me. Please don't wish me away. I'm you. I'm part of you. I am the ugly part of you that you despise. I am the shadow part that loves you even when you scream at me and tell me I'm ugly and you hate me. I am the part of you that needs love. Please send me more love."

I will sit with myself as I continue to write and send this core aspect part of myself more love.

I see a white column of light coming down from the Heavens, with scrubbing bubbles of love and light. It's going through my entire energy field, body, and light body while lighting up the core of my being. It's an intense energy feeling as if a solar storm is knocking out my body.

I have a few choices at this point. I can be in fear of the emotions rising within. I can run to something to numb it. Or I can love it. What we love softens. It's when we resist that it will persist. Today I choose to send the core of my being divine love. And when that happens, I am reset and rewired. I am being flooded with love and light. It's a cooling energy to calm my nerves. I see this blue and white light energy entering my spinal column and out through every nerve ending from there, going out to my every cell. It's like every cell is getting a love bomb!

It transforms and relaxes each cell. It's calming my nervous system outward from the core of my being. My vibration has been reset, and I can breathe much easier. The entire dark night of the soul may not be over, but whatever small part this episode held in my experience, it is complete.

When my heart is heavy, it is my first indication that something is off. At this point my soul is beginning to whisper messages that I am ignoring. As I tune into my body, I ask myself, "What is "pinging" for attention?" Right now, it's my heart chakra. Whenever I feel off, I pray and meditate while asking what I'm sensing. In this instance, I hear this heart heaviness will go away when I finish this book. I am praying that it lets up way before that! It's an aching, awful feeling. Something is literally "on my heart" I need to share. And I am pouring out my heart to you.

I continue to write what messages I receive:

My heart area feels full and heavy. I see the energy as a jagged edge and a black blob of heaviness, heartache, lessons, grief, and more. It's coming up for clearing. It's coming to my attention now to be handled. To be seen, to be loved, and released.

It may want to tell me something. There may be something I need to know. Right now, my heart is racing and pumping at a rapid rate. Not unusual when I'm getting ready to clear something big. I tune in again.

Dear beautiful, courageous body and heart, please talk to me. What is going on that you are suffering so?

And this is the message I receive back, "*Hello there, Miss Lara. We are you. You are us. You are all of it, whether good, bad, negative, or positive. This particular aspect of you is from an ancient part that was hurt long ago. You held it tight in your heart area for this entire life, and now, because it's time to release it — to pour your heart out— it is coming to your attention. You know how it works. Encoded in you is everything you will ever need. We encourage you to pour your heart out on the computer through your words.*"

What does it look like? If I could touch it, what would it feel like? Depending on its location, I may be able to bring in the other senses as well —hearing, tasting, and smelling. In this case, not so much. A black blob of energy has overtaken my entire heart chakra. It is like a front plate and goes deep into my body. Not through the back of my heart, but definitely to my spine. It has jagged edges, in black/dark grayish with spots of red. Red is generally anger or frustration. It's not new, but it's a new sensation to me. These different energies come up when they are ready to be released. This can be frustrating, but the timing isn't always up to us.

Often I will wrap the black energies with love and light and return to Spirit. This time, I am being asked to hold off. Play in this energy and let it pour out of my heart onto the screen. Again, I continue to tune in deeper.

It feels heavy and dark. This particular energy doesn't necessarily have a name or function other than a conglomeration of various hurts ready for healing. My heart feels burdened. It's like I am carrying a heavy backpack in front of my body, and I can't remove it. I want to throw it off. I am having trouble breathing, yet I must keep walking uphill hundreds of miles, huffing and puffing. Anger is building. My heart hurts. It hurts for myself and others. I know this can be removed quickly and effortlessly, but I am not being allowed. I am being asked to sit with it. I am being asked to feel it to the depths of my soul. In the meantime, I attract all the ick it represents in my life. I think of everything that is the most upsetting to me. I do this work every single day. I know many of you do this as well. And, yet, your life still doesn't look like you want.

I hear from others that if you clear this one more thing, you will have what you desire. Make this last move, and everything you have ever dreamed of will be there. And, honestly, it simply isn't true. I get tired of hearing this. I get close, and the goalpost gets moved. The carrot gets pushed further and further from me. I'm exhausted, and at this point, I want to stop. To give up. And, yet, something inside of me won't allow that either. So, I continue. I am dragging my heavy backpack uphill. Tears are falling—anger is building. I am attracting more and more cray-cray while friends fall away. And, family members burn with rage at me for leaving them. As I'm on my long hike of life, it also feels like people are throwing their stuff into my backpack for me to handle for them.

Just because life isn't looking how you want it to doesn't mean you are on the wrong track or have picked up a dark energy. It could be the exact opposite. Our ways are not God's. Everything, and I mean everything, is being used for our or others' soul growth. The undesired circumstances often prepare you for the next level in your soul evolution. Usually, when your soul is experiencing a dark night, the sunrise is closer than you know.

My father-in-law had passed away unexpectedly; soon after, my mother-in-law suffered a debilitating stroke and came to live with us. My husband and I had always planned on her coming to live with us as she aged. I cared for her the best I could. Even with all my own medical and hospice volunteer training, though, I soon learned I was unequipped to care for an aging loved one while running a household, a business, volunteer responsibilities, and an unplanned construction project after our finished basement flooded. Repairs began, and my mother-in-law became more depressed by the day. She would lay on our couch crying daily, asking me why God hadn't taken her yet. I had no answers for her. To add to the pile of stress, I was having health challenges of my own. Both my mental and physical health were declining at a rapid rate. Taking care of myself was always at the bottom of the list. I would have to wait.

In the meantime, after much discussion, we moved my mother-in-law, Doris, into an assisted living facility less than a mile from us. She soon began to perk up, enjoying her new home. She smiled daily, especially when her new friends called her Dancing Doris. She lived another five healthy, happy years enjoying daily cocktail hour, feeling like she was on a cruise ship every day!

Although she flourished in her new home, I felt like a failure. Even with consistent counseling, my marriage of 25 years was falling apart, my health was deteriorating at a record rate, depression consumed me, my hair was falling out, and my kids were making bets on what organ mom would have surgically removed next.

Life can throw us curve balls, knocking us flat on the ground. No one is immune to being side-swiped. My sons recently arrived to work one morning to find their tech company closing that day. A job providing for them and their families was gone instantly—homes and bills to pay with suddenly no income. For one of my sons, that same month, their entire electric system blew in his house (added colossal expense), and a Category 4 hurricane hit his home a couple of weeks later.

I heard myself repeating those old sayings, "When it rains, it pours." And bad things come in three's. Finally, one afternoon, I stopped putting such negative thoughts out to the Universe. I know better, yet when you start getting knocked down, it's easy to let the negativity in. Whenever I hear my head taking a direction that isn't quite the present positivity I want to experience, I say, CANCEL CANCEL, CLEAR CLEAR, and reroute my thinking to something more positive.

Before my kids lost their jobs, I had been praying that they are in divine alignment with their highest potential. Prayer is powerful! Shhhhhhhhh…. Don't tell my kids my prayers may have been why they were both rerouted in their careers!

In just a few days of praying that powerful prayer for myself, I can't even begin to describe the many shifts —from people and opportunities exiting my life and more. I felt 100% aligned with my souls' calling, yet, there's always more to release. The transitions were abrupt and unexpected, some quite painful. All in all, I know without a doubt, these shifts are making room for what my soul asks and requires, my highest potential/ highest destiny and the perfect plan for my life.

I do not have to know the WHERE or WHEN of it. Showing up in surrender and allowing the Divine Plan to arrive is all that is asked. And now, on the other side of many times of getting the rug pulled out from under me, I see the incredible benefits of those times.

- ~ it humbles me. I am reminded that I am NOT God, nor do I play one on TV. His ways are bigger than mine, and I am not to know the why of everything
- ~ we feel more apt to ask for help
- ~ we see the fragility of life. It's a reminder to be in the moment and appreciate even the small things in life
- ~ we get to reinvent ourselves depending on the circumstances, like a job loss

I've noticed that life moves in cycles, including income, healing, love, and business. During times when things are going fantastic, well, enjoy it, is all I can say! Relish that you are reaping the rewards of seeds planted years and even generations before. Be grateful for the abundance while understanding this is a cycle of prosperity. Honoring the moment of flow strengthens you to stand firm when the winds of change choose to blow into your life, be it ever so lightly or a hurricane.

It is easy to be positive and loving when things go our way. Money flows in; we have fun date nights with our partner, the children behave, and our health is excellent. Loved ones are happy. Although I pray and meditate daily, it's within the experience of a dark night of the soul that shit gets real. It's easy to pray when things are going smoothly and you feel great. It's effortless not to be triggered when you are feeling incredible. But what if you are slapped with an energy that couldn't get you out of a wet paper bag?

> "So when you're on your knees, and answers seem so far away
> You're not alone, stop holding on and just be held
> Your world's not falling apart; it's falling into place
> I'm on the throne; stop holding on and just be held
> Just be held, just be held."

As I stare out of my usual window seat on Delta for yet another flight takeoff alone, I start my regular music playlist to calm myself.

> "You're not alone; stop holding on and just be held
> Your world's not falling apart; it's falling into place."

Tears begin to fall. I wipe my cheeks, hoping the passenger beside me doesn't notice.

> "I'm on the throne; stop holding on and just be held
> Just be held, Just be held."

I am reminded by these lyrics that although life may look like a pile of chopsticks to me, it must be deconstructed to construct something new. We live in a physical world that is heavy and dense. Sometimes even dark and angry. To create what we want here on Earth, we must first create it in the spiritual world with visualization co-creating with Source.

On a larger scale, the entire world is shifting. We are all in the process of a giant Jenga game. Similarly, when you move from one house to another, things get messy until you reach your destination to unpack and reorganize. In the meantime, you trip over boxes, can't find items, and feel like you are losing your mind! You sort—keep, garbage, or give away. You may also decide what to keep in your life and what needs to go. As your soul expands, your earthly life will demand a change. It has to align with your updated soul desires. This is why so many people on Earth are shifting houses, jobs, friends, partners, food; you name it. All is shifting in our lives. It has to match our new vibrations. The problem comes in when we are resisting this change.

Although I suspect you would agree we want to see a new earth created and raise our frequencies, we certainly didn't expect our entire lives to be turned upside down and inside out. Can't we keep our old lives and add the new high-vibe shiny life? I wish! I had a client ask me once, "If I start to work with you will I lose my friends?"

Most of us prefer predictably while resisting change. We want the status quo, same-ole comfortable, predictable life that we are leading. Especially if we are a type-A personality that relishes being in control. We have a schedule to abide by. When raising my kids, I thought I could keep a spotless house with two toddlers. I believed I could hold a schedule; if I strayed, something was wrong with me. I worshipped my Franklin Covey Planner (it's a 90's thing). Crossing off to-dos while highlighting in different colors gave me that happy high while my dopamine shot through the roof. Dinner should be on the table at 6 p.m. every night while we all sat happily discussing our days. I also thought I could be a full-time entrepreneur, run a household, volunteer, and care for anyone who called. Buried deep was a belief that if I did good, nothing bad would happen. If I kept peace at all costs (the motto of a child of an alcoholic), all would be well. I believed life should be easier. And I would get very frustrated when it wasn't!

It's not that I had a Pollyanna viewpoint of life. If anything, I was more of a Negative Nelly. The old soul that I am believes life should be easier. And, I desperately beat myself up (with my negative thoughts) when it wasn't. I thought I was DOING something wrong and that I WAS WRONG at the core.

Mastering my energy field and understanding how to shift various other energy fields, including my properties, land, businesses, etc., has allowed me an entirely new perspective on shifting. Most of the time, it will get messy before it can be organized with a higher vibration. It can come back together. The land or life must be cleared of the old toxic debris before there is space for a new higher vibe energy.

And during that time when you're in the transitional shift, you question everything, especially your very existence. It may even feel like a very dark night of the soul. Caring for yourself during a dark night of the soul is crucial for navigating the challenging and transformative experience. Here are some suggestions on how to care for yourself during this time:

1. Self-Compassion: Be gentle and kind to yourself. Please recognize that the dark night of the soul is a difficult period, and it's okay to feel lost or confused—practice self-compassion by treating yourself with understanding, patience, and acceptance.

2. Seek Support: Reach out to trusted friends, family members, or professionals who can provide emotional support and understanding. Consider finding a therapist, counselor, or spiritual guide who can offer guidance and help you navigate the process.

3. Self-Reflection: Engage in self-reflection practices such as journaling, meditation, or contemplation. These practices can help you gain insights into your experiences, emotions, and thoughts and promote a deeper understanding of yourself.

4. Self-Care: Prioritize self-care activities that nourish your physical, mental, and emotional well-being. This can include getting enough rest, eating nutritious meals, exercising regularly, and engaging in activities that bring you joy and relaxation.

5. Nature and Solitude: Spend time in nature, if possible, as it can be grounding and soothing. Additionally, find moments of solitude for introspection and reflection. Disconnecting from external distractions can help you connect with your inner self and facilitate inner growth.

6. Creative Expression: Explore creative outlets such as art, writing, music, or dance. These forms of expression can help channel your emotions, release pent-up energy, and provide a sense of catharsis.

7. Mindfulness and Spirituality: Engage in mindfulness practices or explore spiritual practices that resonate with you. This might involve meditation, prayer, or engaging with philosophical or spiritual texts that provide comfort and inspiration.

8. Patience and Trust: The dark night of the soul is a transformative process that takes time. Practice patience and trust in the journey, knowing that it has the potential to lead to greater self-understanding, growth, and spiritual connection.

It's important to note that everyone's experience during a dark night of the soul is unique, and what works for one person may not work for another. Listen to your needs and intuition, and adapt these suggestions to suit your circumstances. If the dark night of the soul becomes overwhelming or you experience severe distress, don't hesitate to seek professional help.

Now It's Your Turn!

I'm not going to share a meditation for a dark night of the soul! When you are "in it" the LAST thing you want to do is meditate. It's hard enough to even get out of bed. The best thing you can do is follow the suggestions above, beginning with an enormous amount of self-compassion. Journaling, walking in nature, and salt baths are my top three most soul-soothing activities I partake in when I'm feeling down. Loving on yourself while you are going through a dark night is the greatest act of self-compassion. And, as my dear friend Mary Burkhart said "Self-love is not a luxury, but a necessity for health, happiness, and fulfillment." I invite you to give yourself a hug and a break during a dark night of the soul. Say NO more often while you attend to yourself. And, most importantly, know, that this too shall pass.

Scan me

11

Jumping Timelines

> With each thought, feeling, and choice, we are either
> dissolving or strengthening the current timeline
> or creating a new path.
>
> **~Lara Jaye**

A timeline is a trajectory you are on in a specific area of life. It is the direction your train (aka your life path) is headed. It's imperative to know precisely where you want to go and where your train is directed so you don't get derailed or on a train you don't want to be on. Every single area of your life has a timeline attached to it. And, everyone is running numerous timelines all at once. You have a timeline for your work, love life, relationships, home, health, etc. To "jump" timelines implies that you are moving to a new life path. Jumping timelines is a fun way of describing manifesting or designing your destiny. All of these have the same outcome; however, it's up to you to specify if you want to live your highest and most extraordinary life. You create a new timeline with every choice you make; thus, the amount is infinite! If you have a deep desire in your heart, I believe that there is a timeline to support it.

Let's say you are unhappy, unhealthy, lonely, and in a career you despise.

Looking at yourself a few years later, it would be normal to assume all would be going the same. But instead, we see you healthy, fit, energetic, excited about life, with a partner you love, and in a career that fulfills your soul beyond belief. You seem to be living your highest expression of yourself. What happened? You jumped timelines to a different track! You created a new reality. You didn't like how your life was unfolding and chose to allow another series of possibilities to come to fruition. People do this when they "decide" to lose weight, move homes, or switch jobs.

With each thought, feeling, and choice, we are either dissolving or strengthening the current timeline or creating a new path. Often, we sit in the middle of two timelines — the transitory messy chaotic in between. Again, in this spot, with every choice, we are either strengthening the current timeline or creating a new path forward. And so is everyone else. We are often intersecting and sharing timelines with others. If we're not focused on our lane, this can create much confusion.

According to author Kimberly who writes for AreYouAwakening.com, "All possibilities exist in our Universe. Your desire is there waiting for you to focus on it and bring it into view. Can you now see why it's important, if you really, really want something, to stay focused on it? Each time you digress from your desire by thinking a conflicting thought about your goal, you jump onto a different timeline that affects your future. But don't freak out! You can always correct your course by laughing, resending your intentions, and feeling how you'd feel if you had it right now. In one second, you can be back on your desired timeline."[14]

It's way too easy to jump timelines to lower our success. A couple of wrong turns (thoughts and actions), and before we know it, we react rudely to a clerk, drink too much alcohol, or watch Netflix for 12 hours straight.

An up-level in your life or business requires a timeline shift, which begins with a new way of thinking and different choices. Whenever I feel stagnant in an area, I jump timelines to up-level my life. I remind myself that I am never truly stuck and can take my life in any direction. Although I didn't always know it, the power has always been within me! It helps me to remember my favorite quote by Rumi is, "What you seek, is seeking you."

Growing up in the Christian faith, I believed God had a perfect plan for me. I am still figuring out where that dogmatic belief was written. It was just understood. Be a good girl, get married, attend church, have two kids, and live in the suburb with the white picket fence. The typical American dream became my daily focus. My life fit perfectly on an Excel spreadsheet with my Franklin Covey Planner leading the way. And then, I blew it all up by asking for a divorce from my husband. Divorce wasn't in my plan, nor was anything outside of the norm of society I was about to do. Yet, here I was, facing a whole new life. My so-called perfect life plan was in a pile of rubble before me.

The guilt and shame after my divorce were immensely debilitating, and it took me a bit to work through the grief, forgiveness (especially of myself), healing, depression, and more. After I was able to come up for air, I began to see the incredible possibilities for a whole new life before me. A life full of adventure, travel, people, ocean breezes, writing, speaking, and more. All of these things I had dreamt about for years but shoved down into my psyche. I salvaged what was meant to go with me — my children and a few friends — and moved forward slowly yet unapologetically.

The first stop was a big move from a suburb of Indianapolis, Indiana, to the gulf coast beaches of Sarasota, Florida. My oldest son was already working in Florida and planning to move to Japan indefinitely. My youngest was at Indiana University full-time and headed to Spain for the summer. While my family responsibilities were lifting, my focus became re-creating my life. I write extensively about this move in my previous three books in the International Amazon Best Sellers:

More Than Enough: Discover Your Limitless Potential & Live Your Bravest Dream

Midlife Transformation: Redefining Life, Love, Health, & Success

Courageous Heart

Moving homes is only one example of this creation process of jumping timelines. In Chapter 7, I detail my numerous moves. Regardless of where I was moving, there was always a process, and often, it was messy! Even before the actual physical part of moving, there are many other steps in the creation process. I can always tell when I'm getting ready for a massive shift in my life. Does Moses part the Red Sea and angels sing Hallelujah? I wish it were that obvious. Instead, it's quite the opposite. It's like driving for two hours while hitting every red light!

Each move begins with an initial desire within —a nudge from my soul. If I'm not listening, an energetic 2X4 hits me on the head (not literally) to get my attention. Like a potted plant that outgrew her pot, I would feel like I couldn't grow any longer —emotionally or spiritually— unless I got a new "pot!"

As I ponder my next move in any area of my life, I notice that the energy road has ended with whatever I'm doing or where I live. Things start to fall apart all around me. I lose hope. I feel stuck. I don't get the intuitive answers I want. Things feel shut down. I feel agitated and frustrated. Seemingly, blocked at every corner, answers are nowhere to be found. If I dare ask intuitive friends, I get answers all over the board. God gives them these somewhat false or misleading answers partly to test me, and sometimes it's just all they can see. See Chapter 3 on false guides and misleading answers for more on that topic.

Recently, I had another one of my moments where nothing was working. Frustration was rising, and loneliness was leading the way. I knew I needed to ask different questions. The questions I was asking of Spirit weren't getting answers that made sense, and I knew that the questions needed to change.

Instead of, "Where is the highest and best place for me to move to next?" I needed to back it up. I need to dive deeper and make room in my energy field for the next step.

New questions I began to ask were:

What's right about this (not knowing what's next) that I need to see?

What step am I missing that needs to happen first?

Well, the longer I go without a vision, the more agitated I get! Proverbs 29:18 says. "Where there is no vision, the people perish." I began to feel frustrated, anxious, troubled, and lonely. When this happens, I usually sit in it for several days instead of remembering what to do. Then, something triggers me to ask different questions.

I go deeper. What is under these lower energy and vibrational emotions I was feeling? I desire a deeper connection.

I took each emotion I was feeling one by one. I dove deeper into my body and my feelings. I wanted to know where it lived in my body. What did it want to tell me, if anything? I blessed it, wrapped it in love, and sent it on its way. By morning, I felt lighter. I felt like I had made so much space in my body and energy field that answers flowed effortlessly into me.

There was somewhere for the answers to go! There was somewhere for the higher vibe energy to go! I felt terrific – light and fresh. As I dove deeper into myself, I envisioned myself diving off a high dive into my being. I pretended to swim around. I was looking for the loneliness and the stuck emotions.

I stopped when I found each emotion, including talking to them and swimming around. It felt freeing. It felt good. I connected deeper to myself. I made room in myself for a higher vibrational timeline. Yesterday the answer I got was different than today. Why? Because my energy frequency was different. I had released more stuck emotions and allowed a new higher vibe to enter my cells. If you want the highest frequency timelines, we must keep clearing our energy field daily. As I allowed myself to release that which was holding me back, it made more room in my energy field for a higher frequency answer.

I just described the beginning of the inner work to find that new timeline and new desire within myself. Without doing the inner work, we continue the status quo, and nothing ever changes because we are not shifting anything within ourselves. As we shift our energy and our inner psyche, we make room for a higher vibrational timeline to enter.

In the past, I would look outside myself for answers on every aspect of my life's who, what, where, and when. My engrained belief in 'God's Plan' and my not wanting to mess it up any more than I already had, made me very cautious moving forward. Although my family would argue that I make huge, fast-moving decisions, they do not know the lamenting and prayer that goes into each choice, and I usually share with them after the fact as the boxes are being packed.

Typically, it's best not to share our thoughts and dreams with others. Well-meaning friends and family may sabotage us, diluting our dreams down to dust. We begin to second guess ourselves because others can't see what we see for ourselves. I can always tell if I've over-shared something personal with someone by their reaction and their less-than-encouraging words. Remember, no one else will see or know everything you do about your life and dreams.

Instead of feeling shame because I'm off God's plan, I believe we have much free will on how we want to reach our destination. Arthur Ashe said, "Success is a journey, not a destination." Our dreams for our highest potential are embedded in us. And, as we look within, it will guide us to our ultimate destination as we weave our free will of choices along the journey. Life isn't a straight line of perfection; it progresses after a few steps forward and several back. Don Williams says, "The road of life twists and turns, and no two directions are ever the same. Yet our lessons come from the journey, not the destination."

I visualize jumping on a new train to get to my next destination. This new train is taking me to the next stop in my life. I have a clear intention that this train has all I desire as the highest expression of myself, my highest potential. I am at peace, living in joy, and surrounded by love and a supportive community. I see myself on this train, waking up happy and healthy each morning. I smile as I encounter the beautiful souls of my family and loved ones nearby. I dance with joy with my loving divine partner. I define what I'd like my environment to look like and especially how I'd like to feel. I see myself living my best life while making the most significant impact on others. And I also leave room for co-creation with Spirit by saying, "Or something better!"

As I tune in most mornings to this new timeline train, I continue to observe and ask questions of Spirit for more details. Not necessarily to learn what the future could hold (although that is fun), but mostly to see where I need to be aligned with the future frequencies. For example, do I look or eat differently in my highest expression? I ask for specific details. I want to know how I look as this person, what I am eating, whom am I hanging out with, what does my work look like, and what does my home look and feel like? And, most importantly, how can I integrate these new frequencies into the current me?

Everything created on the physical plane has an energetic signature, designed first and foremost in the spiritual realm or quantum, as scientists refer to the creation point. That is exactly what visualization and meditation do — they create the form of what we desire and allow us to connect with its blueprint frequencies. With each morning, I visualize, I am calling in the new frequencies, connections, and opportunities to align with this new me. Depending on what it is, how many energetic blocks we have to receive it, free will, and divine timing determine when the train arrives!

To move homes, the process begins with what I described above — visualization and prayer. What area best fits my needs? What even are my needs and desires? Finding a new home can be energetically and physically exhausting and exhilarating all at the same time! There is a tear-down (packing) time, a transition (driving from one location to another), and then a rebuilding (unpacking and organizing) time. Each phase can take a few days to up to a year. Whether the move is down the road or across the country, to process it emotionally takes time to release the current home, be in the messy transition, and welcome the new house.

Some moves were more challenging than others. Of course, letting go of the family home in Indiana was extra emotionally challenging. All the happy memories of raising the kids were etched in the walls. For every house I leave, I take time after everything is packed and spend a few moments thanking the house for supporting me. I ask that it return all my happy memories to go with me and say a special blessing to the new owner.

During the transition period of actual transportation from one house to another, I continue to release the past residents, sending blessings and welcoming in the new. I envision who I will be in this new house. I see my lifestyle and how I want to live in the new place. Unless it's a move in the same city, this is a couple-of-week process while my pod arrives at the new spot. I take this time seriously, to rest while preparing emotionally and physically for unpacking and beginning anew.

Interestingly enough, after I threw out my Excel spreadsheet and Franklin Covey Planner, I realized the power within to create my destiny. My life has opened up to new adventures I couldn't have planned or predicted. It's imperative to know what direction I want to go and, simultaneously, leave room for flexibility for God to weave in additional detours, blessings, and miracles along the way. That is true Co-Creating with the Universe!

And, While You WAIT…

When jumping timelines, we design our lives how we want them. As we become more self-aware, our dreams become more evident. We begin to dream bigger and bigger, realizing it's up to us to co-create with the Universe on our highest potential and destiny. We follow all the steps to jump to that new life (listed below) and go to sleep, dreaming of living our highest expression that will arrive in the morning when we awake. And, when we open our eyes and look around —— it's all more of the same.

What did I do wrong?

What do I need to do differently?

I should have asked for something else. Something smaller, perhaps.

I hate waiting! What can I do to speed things up?

Do any of these questions sound familiar? I've asked myself these questions on more than one occasion.

The WAIT for your dream to come to fruition can be one of your life's most challenging times.

You may have big dreams. Dreams like creating a profitable and sustainable business. You have poured into it for years, and it's still not taking off. Or you may want to meet that special someone. Yet for years, dating has seemed like a bad joke at your expense. Or are you and your partner struggling to get pregnant? Each month arrives with a "negative" line appearing, as if you will never hold your child.

Your heart and body ache for your dream. Well-meaning friends say, "Well, you should stop trying, and it will come to you." Of course, their comments only frustrate you more. And yet another year passes with an unfilled dream etched in your soul.

In the meantime, frustration rises in you. You wonder if you should give up.

I know those feelings all too well. Years ago, I experienced one of the circumstances I mentioned above. Utter devastation would encompass me every month when I learned I wasn't pregnant, and I would be curled up in a ball on the bathroom floor, crying in deep grief for yet another month of an unfilled dream.

I knew I was meant to have children. I would ask myself with tears streaming down my face, "Why wasn't it happening? What is wrong with me? What am I doing wrong?" I felt like a failure, while thinking my body was failing me.

Eventually, after a year, I got pregnant with my first child. And, soon after, my second son. Looking back (they are 30 and 28), I can see the perfect timing of their arrival.

And now, as I wait for other dreams to come to fruition, I have to practice what I learned long ago.

1. Practice gratitude.
   Pour into your journal, prayers, and meditations how grateful you are for exactly where you are right now. List everything in your life that is there. Be thankful for this waiting season in your life. It will help you see the many blessings so that even more can come.

2. Practice impeccable self-care.
   Pour into yourself. Love yourself as you've never loved yourself. You deserve it. You've been given a colossal dream bubbling up in your body. Your body must be honored, respected, and loved during this trying time. Take care of yourself intellectually (watch your mind chatter), emotionally (handle your emotions as they arise—do not numb or stuff them back down), and physically (take daily walks in nature, practice restorative yoga, and nourish your body with healthy foods, and energetically (get rid of toxic people and drama in your life).

3. Do one thing.
   Do one thing each day that gets you ready to receive your dream. Are you waiting on a child? Sew a baby blanket. Are you creating that business to serve others? Start doing what you love today, whether you get paid or not. Waiting to meet

someone special? Often we're so busy that there needs to be more space for others to squeeze themselves into our too-busy lifestyle. Make room for that desired partner by cutting out an unnecessary activity.

4. Get busy acting as if.
While being grateful and practicing impeccable self-care, act as if you are already living your dream. Whatever that is, go about your day as if it's already here. How would you act differently? Would you whine about how you don't have something? No, you would write in your gratitude journal how thankful you are that you are with your child. Or that you're serving in your profitable soulful business. Or you're grateful for time with your beloved. Whatever it is you're hoping for, begin to act as if you already have it. Notice your body relax. Notice your demeanor change to joy. Notice your smile return to your face.

5. Repeat positive affirmations such as:
Everything is always working out fantastic for me.
I always manifest my dreams quickly and effortlessly.

6. Surrender the HOW and WHEN.

I want to reassure you that you are not forgotten if you are still waiting for something to come to fruition. If it's a material item, such as a car or clothes, I've found it is much easier to manifest than another person because free will is involved.

Co-creating with God is a delicate dance of surrender, detachment, and holding space. I want this thing, I'm holding space for it, I envision myself having this thing, yet I trust and release it to Spirit to allow it to "show up" at the perfect time and in an ideal way. This is co-creating with Spirit at its finest. Letting go of the attachment to

Jumping Timelines

the item, surrender to the HOW and WHEN "it" shows up while trusting. Easier said than done!

Waiting for the Universe game can be compared to ordering a steak dinner. Five minutes later, you realize it's still not sitting before you. Believing you need to ask for something smaller, cheaper, or easier to cook, you call the waitress back to change your order while cooking the steak. The waitress returns to the kitchen to say the customer changed their mind and would like the chicken wings on the menu instead.

At this point, you are probably getting a tad "hangry" (angry/hungry) waiting on your wings, even though the steak was almost ready. And now the wait is even longer! As you sit at the restaurant waiting, you are using that time to envision yourself eating the fantastic piece of chicken, although it wasn't exactly what you wanted in the first place. You try not to fill yourself with bread at the table, but it's ever so tempting. Even though you can't see it, you trust your meal is being cooked behind the closed kitchen door. You are holding the vision. You don't know when it's coming, but you are eagerly waiting.

When there is a delay in what we desire to materialize, we must trust that God knows the bigger picture of perfect timing. We don't know what's happening behind the scenes in the kitchen! We don't know the reorganization of energy, people, circumstances, and events that need to occur for you to receive what you are asking for.

Ideally, we will go through these steps to dream our most prominent dream. Then we will surrender the HOW and WHEN, while trusting all is in perfect order. Lastly, get busy doing something else! To co-create doesn't mean we control it all; it means we allow Spirit to make His moves on our behalf. Our job now is to rest in the known and unknown. Know that your fantastic meal is being cooked in the kitchen. Items are being set up for you to be served on this fantastic, beautiful plate. And it will exceed your desires because the chef in the kitchen knows an even better way of making whatever you ordered, especially if you clarified, "or something better!"

Our dreams etched in our very being will come to fruition at the right time. The right time though, isn't up to us. In the meantime, you know what to do while you wait, expecting joyfully.

Now It's Your Turn!

Scan the QR Code below to hear Lara guide you through a deep light language meditation to jump to a new timeline. Have a pen and paper ready to journal your thoughts.

Know exactly what you desire in each area of your life. Utilize self-awareness techniques to dive deep into the divine design of your life. It's not enough to know what we don't want. Instead, stay focused on what you desire. If you are unsure, ask Spirit to guide you to the highest expression of yourself living in peace, love, and joy.

Continue to do this visualization as often as you'd like! If you feel resistance, ask your Spirit Team to help you raise your frequency to match your desired experience and request that all older timelines and interference energies be dissolved. And, get busy enjoying your current life! There is nothing like the NOW moment that creates the next moment.

12

Sweet Emotions

Sweet emotion Sweet emotion
You talk about things that nobody cares
Wearing out things that nobody wears
You're calling my name but I gotta make clear
I can't say, baby, where I'll be in a year

~Aerosmith

Even without my imaginary friend alongside me, spirituality had always been my passion. I didn't want to miss church when I was a little girl. I received something special there that helped me through the week ahead. My grandparents took me to the Auburn Presbyterian Church in Northern Indiana when they were in town. When I could drive myself, I would meet my grandparents on the pew, volunteer, acolyte, and participate in youth group. Although my immediate family members thought I was nuts for wanting to be involved, I continued. It filled that hole in my heart like nothing else.

Eventually, attendance and volunteering at church replaced any communication with Spirit, my guides, and angels. I prayed a lot—which meant I was doing a lot of talking and not much listening. After getting married at 21, my husband and I relocated to a suburb of Indianapolis,

Indiana. I began teaching Bible studies at our local Methodist Church, co-led a mom's group, and volunteered six days a week until my health began to suffer. God was my rock—leading and guiding me. However, the more I worked at the church, the more I saw the imperfections in the system. People were fighting and disagreeing everywhere I turned. Committees were formed to accomplish great things, yet came to a standstill due to differing opinions.

As preschoolers, my children attended our church's preschool, and it was "J" week. They were highlighting J and the word Jello. When I asked the director why not use the word Jesus for J week, I was scolded and put in my place that there was no way she would allow her teachers to talk about Jesus because she didn't want to offend anyone. I don't know about you, but I would assume the church preschool curriculum will include a few Jesus teachings. Goodness, if we can't talk about Jesus in church, where can we? Although the director didn't allow any immediate changes, within a couple of years, J week was now all about Jesus and not Jello! My heart was happy!

As I look back at all the lessons I learned at church (that frankly had nothing to do with God or the Bible), I learned about people. Everyone has their own story they project to the world, and buried beneath the surface are the rumblings of a volcano. It's a given that any place where you are in intimate connection with others, you will come against other opinions, and you will be triggered. Thank them — they are your greatest teachers.

One such occasion, I was at my wit's end working in the church office, seeing the hypocritical discrepancies. I did something that took me years to forgive myself. I suspect a few others still haven't forgiven me. I wrote a letter and presented it to an office staff member outlining everything I felt this person was doing wrong and being done to me.

Although there's no excuse for what I did, looking back I can see clearly what happened. What I didn't understand at the time, as I worked in the office (a job I loved, by the way), every single problem, issue, and complaint that came through I heard, felt, and internalized. Member after member issue, plus staff complaints and hardness of life, meant I was wiped. As a sensitive empath, my body took on these heavy issues. I had no idea what was happening other than I felt awful whenever I left the church office. I could barely function. The emotions filled my body like a balloon; when it finally popped, it was an explosion.

My husband and I had been church members for over 20 years. After this incident and one other strange occurrence, our family left the Methodist church forever. It was bittersweet —devastating and relieving at the same time— to walk away from the four walls that once supported and loved our family. Although I've apologized to that office staff member in writing and in person several times, I don't know if she ever truly forgave me. And I do not blame her.

At the time, blowing up was the only way I knew how to process emotions. This isn't something we are taught in school. Hard lessons such as this are our greatest teachers. Regardless of why I did what I did, I am responsible for processing my own emotions and preferably in a way that doesn't project or harm others. I finally began to take time to process these pent-up emotions —whether they were mine or others and move them through. Other than yelling, I found ways to heal my broken parts.

After this explosive episode at church, I dove into myself to learn how to manage my emotions. There were so many things going on in my life — including depression, health issues, facing a possible separation, and more. I knew that I needed to figure myself out before I hurt anyone else in the process.

Sweet Emotions

I began to question my faith. Soon after, my husband and I were separated, the nest was emptying, and I sold my marketing company. My hair was falling out in clumps, my body hurt everywhere, and I was very depressed. As I walked away from the four walls of a church building, I went within to actually meet the God that lived in me. I gave up my rushing around my do-do-do life to just BE.

My physical and emotional pain was unbearable after years of grasping onto emotions and beliefs that no longer served me. Finally, I parked myself on my couch, meditating, praying, and writing to unravel the knots that had plagued me for decades. At my lowest point, I realized the power was within me all along. Angels would appear and channel what is called Light Language. Memories flooded back to me as a child, writing, speaking, and hand-signing this language. My health began to improve significantly. My clarity and zest for life returned soon after.

I was hooked. And at the same time, I hid.

I struggled with what was happening. My head couldn't understand what I was saying, nor could I explain the purpose or even name it. Intuitively, I knew my Language came from the Angels. Often I would refer to it as "Angel Speak," for lack of a better name. Questions continued to float through my head, like:

What would people think?

What am I saying?

Would I start blurting this out while in line at the grocery?

I didn't have any answers.

Fast forward several years…Honestly, I didn't want anyone to know about this gift. This secret power. This woo-woo part of me that often wasn't accepted in my suburban, corporate life. As the years went by, I knew this gift couldn't be kept quiet anymore. My soul was screaming at me to be heard. I began to see a place for me in the world being ME — both a corporate and a spiritual woman. I didn't have to separate the spiritual part of me from the business aspect. I began to see how the two could be beautifully merged.

It was time for me to come out of the closet.

I learned in my quiet stillness to communicate with Source, my higher self, and angelic energies and, for the last decade, show others how to do the same. Hundreds of clients, thousands of meditations, and several books later, I am still in awe of Heaven's precise, loving guidance.

Light Language doesn't speak to our heads. Instead, it bypasses our heads (and ego) and goes straight to our hearts. This is the Language of our heart and soul. This is a language that is not understood at the physical level. However, our souls soak up the words and the codes it contains. It is truly LIGHT Language. It carries LIGHT from God, our Source. It carries codes and imprints straight from the heavens to all of us for our own healing and many other purposes.

Light Language will speak to your soul and allow your soul to speak back so that your next steps are clear, enlightened, and inspired. Not everyone who speaks Light Language brings in the same codes and imprinting, so I can only speak to what I know I am doing. My Light Language is specifically designed for these unique purposes:

- Reorganization of energy–It moves stuck energy and emotions
- Activates people to realize their unlimited potential
- Clears and balances chakras
- Upgrades DNA

- Imprints healing and regenerating codes
- Repairs holes and tears in auric fields
- Imprints a higher vibration into cells
- Recalibrates the body and energy field
- Clear unhealthy cords and bonds to people, places, things, circumstances
- All of the above for animals, homes, land, and any space, as well

Light Language is ancient and sacred. It's not something to take lightly, yet it can be used as often as needed or desired. I'm honored and thrilled to be able to share this powerful, transformative, and divine gift from the Heavens. As I'm working on clients, what it does for them, it does for me as well. It moves stuck energy like nothing I've ever seen.

Listening to Light Language can profoundly impact our mood and clarity level and even our ability to make better decisions. Listening can quickly shift a situation and foster extraordinary balance and extreme clarity. When we communicate with those energies and lead from this place, we can master the invisible and our physical world. Light Language is a form of communication that transcends the boundaries of language and logic. It is a multidimensional language that can be expressed through sound, symbols, and movement. I speak it, hand sign it, write, dance, and paint Light Language. You can as well! Light Language is used to raise your energy and vibration. It is an energetic language that can be expressed in various forms, such as sounds, symbols, and movements.

When I first began understanding what Light Language is (a form of speaking in tongues), I knew only a handful of people who did this in a public setting. As I write this, thousands of people are being activated every day to the power of this Language. Meditation, writing, prayer, Light Language, and consistent spiritual practices all contributed to my healing first, then others' emotional and physical issues.

Healing the Triggers

Those unprocessed emotions are under the surface, ready to be poked. You may be thinking about all the times that you "all of a sudden" felt off. Only when I slowed down enough to feel the stuck emotions while getting to the root of the trigger was I able to heal.

To be triggered is to experience an emotional or physical reaction to something. People could trigger us. A smell. A place. A substance. A song. It could be anything that is a reminder of something intense that happened to us. Triggers are easily identifiable by our reactions. Most of us know what triggers us. Often, we're caught off guard. You know you're experiencing a trigger by how you react to something. What shows up in your life that happens over and over that you react to? How does it affect you? And others around you? Generally, we're quite reactionary.

Examples of circumstances that could trigger you:

- An unexpected bill in the mail
- A comment from someone
- People not showing up for their appointed time
- People showing up late
- Being overcharged

These are just a few examples. Hundreds, if not thousands, of people, places, smells, comments, and circumstances could trigger any of us. We are all walking around with open wounds, just waiting to be healed.

Steps to Heal the Trigger

    1. Accept responsibility and allow awareness to come forth. Begin to see the situation with a wider perspective. What is my role in this situation?

    2. Name it. What's the feeling that I'm experiencing? Is it

abandonment? Is it greed? Loneliness? When was the first time I remember feeling this feeling?
3. Place it. Where do I feel it in my body? Our bodies hold cellular memory of the past. These situations come along in our lives to help us shake loose those stuck emotions.
4. Turn it around. Where am I _____? Fill in the blank of where you are abandoning yourself, not showing up for, not honoring, and respecting yourself. Generally, we attract what we are being; however, this is only sometimes the case. Give yourself grace while you observe if a narcissist or gaslighting situation is at hand.

The world is a reflection of what's going on inside of us. What's your world showing you about yourself? What does it want you to see? Or what does it want you to have awareness about? It's not about beating yourself up. It's about getting quiet and becoming aware, going inward and examining. This is maturity. This is EQ—-emotional intelligence. EQ is the capacity to be aware of control, express your emotions, and handle interpersonal relations judiciously and empathetically. EQ is the key to both personal and professional success. It's not reacting. When I finally slowed down enough to catch my breath and reconnect to myself, I could allow the door to open for deep healing.

It always begins with stillness and awareness.

In the calmness, ask yourself, WWLD? What Would LOVE Do? What would it look like if I led with LOVE in all I did? What would you LOVE to do in this situation I feel triggered in? Triggers make us human, and they are controllable.

I shifted myself from over-working, over-volunteering, and worshiping in a church setting, to diving deeper into Light Language and spiritual practices to support the new me. Spirituality fed my soul and my new practices and disciplines (outlined below) cleared the stuck emotions, allowing for a joyful and healthy new me to emerge.

Coming from the church setting, I pushed the context of spirituality away at first. Only when I actually experienced it for myself did I realize the power in this connection. Spirituality is simply anything that relates to your spirit or soul. We are, first and foremost, spiritual beings having a human experience. To embrace spirituality means opening your heart, allowing and acknowledging that your soul or spirit lives within you. You desire a consistent connection between your soul and your higher self, God, angels or ascended masters, or other beings living in the spirit realm. This connection provides a higher vibration than we usually encounter here on Earth.

What does a Spiritual Practice look like?

A Spiritual Practice is a consistent performance of an action or activity solely to cultivate spiritual development. It's a purposeful habit that allows for an opening within, an acknowledgment of your soul and spirit for connection to yourself, God, and others. My spiritual activities, outlined below, have become an integral part of my daily activities, like taking a shower or brushing my teeth. Aside from providing a respite in my busy life and a necessary life raft for self-preservation, these practices strengthen my resilience in riding life's roller coaster.

Why should I incorporate a Spiritual Practice?

Billions of people around the globe, including moms, dads, children, conscious CEOs, entertainment executives, entrepreneurs, influencers, and leaders worldwide, welcome spirituality to help themselves and their employees professionally and personally. They are embracing a new way to lead and be — authentic, transparent, and connected. They want to be fulfilled from the inside out.

They understand that by expanding their spiritual practices and scope of knowledge, it becomes their EDGE in business and life. It fulfills their soul's yearning while they welcome this powerful and positive edge in life and business. In "A Spiritual Audit of Corporate America," business professor Ian I. Mitroff found that "Spirituality could be the ultimate competitive advantage." This edge comes from developing your spiritual practices (as described below) or allowing a spiritual mentor to advise you in tapping into your intuitive abilities by going within.

Intuition is the ability to understand something immediately without needing conscious reasoning. Everyone is intuitive at some level. The only difference is the inner work needed to become a clear channel to receive the information. Often you will hear someone say, "It was a gut decision" or "I felt it was right." That is their intuition at work. It's a feeling or a clear knowing of what to do. High-powered executives know that learning to tap into their GPS is the key to up-leveling their life and business.

To know thyself is our job. We are 100% responsible for caring for ourselves and knowing ourselves while staying true to our values. No one else can determine our values or beliefs, nor should they! This work is ours and ours alone. This responsibility isn't limited to taking care of our minds, bodies, and spirits. It also encompasses our energy and emotions.

Self-love is not self-indulgence; it's self-preservation.

Often, as life gets busy, we ignore our soul's desire while stuffing emotions and meeting unmet needs with addictions. Fixated cravings on excess sugar, talking, smoking, drugs, gambling, sex, workaholism, or over-exercising drives others away. These act as your shield against the outside world and block you from feeling your emotions. They especially keep you from loving yourself and others. Developing a spiritual practice can help break those addictions while offering undeniable self-love. These practices elevate your self-respect, reminding you to take care of your needs first and to give from the overflow.

Men, women, and young adults from all walks of life seek out spiritual advisors to assist themselves in various ways. They have learned at their core there is a place for spirituality and its practices in their life.

Creative genius and the late CEO of Apple, Steve Jobs, had a well-documented Zen priest as a spiritual advisor. Executive Coach., Jeff Giesea says, "Even Steve Jobs was fundamentally animated by his spirituality. He carried around Paramahansa Yogananda's book, **Autobiography of a Yogi**, since he was a teenager. Copies of it were handed out to guests at his funeral, a detail he no doubt specified in advance." Facebook's guiding light, Mark Zuckerberg, and several other American technology gurus have been drawn to an ashram in India for guidance and teachings.

Leaders worldwide are welcoming spiritual consultants into their companies to help themselves and their employees professionally and personally. Specific religions are generally not discussed. Instead, it's about guiding them to create connections between their values, purpose, and passions in a way they often have yet to think to connect the dots. The result? Greater satisfaction and fulfillment, lower stress, clarity, and improved performance. Executives from various industries gathered at Harvard Business School to discuss how their spirituality helps them be influential leaders. The conference explored issues of leadership, values, and spirituality in business. Most interesting to me were the many different ways each expressed their spirituality. Some spoke of dharma, others finding their primary values, Christian values, reading the Bible at work, and social justice.

According to authors Martha Lagace, Sean Silverthorne, & Wendy Guild of Does Spirituality Drive Success?[15] they write: "For Robert

Glassman, Catalytica Energy Systems, his spirituality at work is expressed as a commitment to social justice. As co-founder and co-chairman of Wainwright Bank & Trust Company based in Boston, Glassman (HBS MBA' 69) said, issues such as homelessness, women's rights, and outreach to the gay and lesbian community had shaped his own life and the life of his business.

Seven years ago, for instance, Wainwright Bank had a quarter of 1 percent of the commercial banking scene in the Boston-Cambridge area, but was financing over 50 percent of AIDS housing, Glassman said. In addition to outreach and socially responsible investing, the bank offers online donation functionality to any nonprofit that is a bank customer—even if all they have is a checking account. The harmony among his personal life, business life, and philanthropy, he said, "is as close as I'm going to come to being a spiritual person." He cited with pride the fact that his daughter works with the Coalition for the Homeless in New York City. "That there is a sense of continuity in the family [is] the most authentic thing I can say about what Wainwright Bank does."

According to Ricardo Levy, chairman of Catalytica Energy Systems, executives are trained for action—contemplation is not part of their rulebook. In his own career, however, he discovered the need for spiritual guidance in crucial decisions, especially those that affect other people such as employees, he said.

Levy's guidelines are:

- Quiet the mind.
- Reach deep inside. Go beyond the ego to hear the inner voice.
- Don't fear ambiguity; rest in the unknown. "This is the most difficult piece," Levy admitted. "We're not comfortable unless we see the path."

- Stay humble in the face of temptation and power. "Being humble is a key issue. It's good for a leader to be reminded of the intoxication of power."

Asked by a member of the audience for his definition of success, Levy said, "I'd rather use the word fulfillment. Success is a metric; you never have enough. But only you can define fulfillment. We as individuals are the only judges."

In the Netflix documentary *Wild Wild Country*, spiritual guru OSHO's personal attorney, Philip Toelkes (aka Swami Prem Niren) says he worked for the "fastest-growing law firm in U.S. I was born to do this. But I was working my ass off. I was f***king toast. I was done. After I got divorced, I thought, what am I doing? Eating, drinking too much, working too much. For what? I decided enough is enough. I resigned my partnership. People thought I was crazy for walking away from the gold mine. So, I went to India. Felt like I had come home."

I believe what Philip and the many other leaders are finding when they personally begin to know themselves, following their guiding inner wisdom, the benefits are immeasurable. They include:

- Extreme clarity
- Expanded intuition
- Balanced life
- Deeper connections (to themselves, others, and God)
- Deeper meaning in their work aligned with their values

Incorporating spiritual disciplines in my everyday life transformed me to receive that extra clarity, intuition, harmonious life, deeper connection, and meaningful life I so desired. To have a spiritual discipline means you are involved in an activity, exercise, or regimen that develops or improves your spirituality. It's like training to connect to your soul.

Spiritual discipline brings your inner and outer beings together and connects you to your own higher power.

People think they need to meditate alone for twelve-plus hours a day to see any improvement. The truth is quite the opposite—even the smallest change in your routine can make a world of difference. All of the practices outlined here can be done today with no special equipment—only a willingness and intention to look within. My personal **Top 8 Spiritual Practices** are:

Be Still. Take a few minutes for yourself before your day starts. Listen to that still, small voice within. Sit quietly with your eyes closed or stare off into the stillness of nature. The time you take for noticing allows your soul to whisper to you.

Offer Gratitude. Breathe deeply and contemplate all the fabulousness in your life. Journal or contemplate as many things you can think of you are thankful for. Offer deep and profound gratitude for all of it. Offer thanks for your expanding bank accounts (whether or not they are growing in the present moment), family, friends, health, and more. Gratitude and appreciation set the stage for a fantastic DAY!

Observe Mental Chatter. As you are still, mind chatter may begin to take over. Begin to pay attention to your thoughts. Once you notice negative thoughts running in the background, you can choose to change them. It all starts with awareness. Continue to think about only that which you want to expand. What we focus on expands. What we resist persists.

Practice Mindfulness. Focus intently on the present moment during various activities like eating, walking, working, talking, yoga, or purposeful breathing. Mindfulness is paying attention to what is before you without judging it. Whatever you are doing, bring all five senses into focus (Sight, Hearing, Taste, Smell, Touch). Voila! You're being mindful! Being mindful alone allows you to develop emotional intelligence (EQ), which is imperative (and proven) to enhance your professional success. According to HelpGuide.org, EQ is being aware of, controlling, and expressing your emotions while handling interpersonal relationships judiciously and empathetically. EQ is another way of looking at spiritual growth. As you understand yourself better, tune into your emotions and recognize the emotions and needs of others.

Pray. Praying is talking to Spirit. Request your needs and desires—whatever you want to create in your life. You can even set intentions for your life. Ask for help with your health and finances for yourself or others. The Bible says, "You have not, because you ask not" (James 4:2-3) and, "Ask, and it shall be given" (Matthew 7:7) NIV.

Meditate—Contemplative. Contemplative Meditation is one form of meditation I practice almost every day. Prayer for me is when I am doing all the talking to God. Meditating is when I get quiet enough to hear what God says. It's a focused intent, concentrated on an object worthy of consideration, such as powerful words. Pick any word—Love, Abundance, Health, Purpose, Jesus, God, Joy, Peace, Patience, Kindness, Wealth, or your choice. Focus only on that word for a few minutes. Feel it. See it. Hear it. Taste it. Bring it into your energy field and feel like you are becoming it. I invite you to go within, and as your mind wanders to your "To Do" list, gently and lovingly bringing your mind back to the word at hand. No judgment. There's no right or wrong way to meditate. No effort is required or needed. It's best to let go of any expectations of how the meditation will be.

Meditate—Create Your Life. I also do this specific meditation first thing in the morning. It sets my day up for success while I'm co-creating my future. You can follow along in the meditation below. You may notice changes in your mental and physical health, including lower stress levels, a healthier immune system, and increased memory, concentration, and energy.

Let's Get Physical. Take a walk, do yoga, or ride a bike—anything to get your body moving. Being responsible for the beautiful masterpiece that is your body is an honor, not drudgery. Bonus points if you walk outside in nature (think sandy beach, park trails, or mountains)! Nature absorbs emotions. So, if you're feeling overloaded emotionally, walk outdoors, even for only fifteen minutes.

If you can implement only one of these spiritual practices, I recommend you begin with either of the meditation practices mentioned above, and here's why: meditation blows away everything I've ever tried to change my life. I have said affirmations, made goals, set intentions, and prayed. And still, I couldn't change important areas of my life. I seemingly consistently failed, feeling worse about myself than before I made changes. The triggers of daily life sent me into a frenzy until I started to meditate.

Meditation cuts through to the patterns already programmed in your subconscious. Those old programs are running the show in your life. You may be trying to change on the surface, but the computer software running the show, your subconscious, isn't going to have it!

Almost immediately, when I began to meditate, I could feel a difference. This simple practice reprogrammed me to live from my soul's purpose instead of what the world says I should do. When you meditate, every cell in your body fills with more energy, which results in joy, peace, and enthusiasm. Old programs running in the background get disabled, so you can meet your goals, eat healthily, and—most importantly—live in the present rather than in reaction mode from your past.

The great news about meditation is that the results are cumulative. The benefits accumulate as you embrace the practice, like when you exercise. When I began meditating, I felt an all-around peace. My thoughts were clearer; my energy was focused. Life had a more effortless ebb and flow. Messages were crystal clear. I began to sense, see, and hear angels. The more I surrendered my agenda, my expectations, and my ego, God was able to speak to me powerfully, and I was able to hear the messages.

According to the EOC Institute, studies show over and over how meditating:

- Strengthens the immune system
- Improves your relationships
- Increases serotonin production
- Improves concentration
- Encourages a healthy lifestyle
- Shrinks problems and brings solutions to mind
- Reduces stress, depression, and anxiety
- Adds clarity and peace of mind
- Lowers blood pressure
- Decreases tension in the body
- Increases the energy level

Meditation means to engage in contemplation, usually with a focused mental intent or a single point of reference. According to *Psychology Today*, "Meditation can involve focusing on the breath, bodily sensations, or a word or phrase known as a mantra. In other words, meditation means turning your attention away from distracting thoughts and focusing on the present moment."

When I first began meditating, I used a guided meditation, which helped me relax while staying focused (YouTube, Calm, or Headspace App). As my skill increased, I could take a few deep breaths before dropping into the space of openness almost instantly.

When I'm seeking guidance on important issues in my life, prayer, and meditation are always my first stop. I invite you to look within your heart for your soul's direction for your life. I can't imagine my life without meditation. My life has transformed mainly due to this one practice alone. Meditation quickly centers me and provides a reset anytime, anywhere. This, too, could be your go-to for reducing the stress in your daily life.

At first, you may see progress in physical relaxation and emotional calmness. Later, you may notice other, subtler changes. Some of the most important benefits of meditation make themselves known over time and are not dramatic or easily observed. Persist in your practice, and you will find that meditation frees you from the worries gnawing at you. By opening up space inside, you can experience the joy of being fully present, here and now. Start with five minutes in the morning and five minutes at night before sleep. This one thing will skyrocket you to a more centered, peaceful life—externally and internally.

Regardless of where you start, I invite you to tune into yourself for a few minutes each morning and evening. This newfound self-awareness will allow stuck emotions to become sweet emotions moving through your psyche, catapulting you to the inner peace your soul craves.

The Wisdom Within

Now It's Your Turn!

Scan the QR Code below to hear Lara guide you through a deep light language meditation to release stuck emotions. Have a pen and paper ready to journal your thoughts.

13

Lonely People

This is for all the lonely people
Thinking that life has passed them by
Don't give up
Until you drink from the silver cup
And ride that highway in the sky

This is for all the single people
Thinking that love has left them dry
Don't give up
Until you drink from the silver cup
You never know until you try

~America

Dating in mid-life can sometimes be fun, thrilling, and downright scary. For a good laugh, friends often want to hear my crazy dating stories. Although I make light of it, much of my dating life has been traumatizing. Many stories are flat-out incomprehensibly insulting and degrading and will never be mentioned unless I'm working on healing something from it. It wasn't very long ago my body would tremble even thinking about dating again. With the mention of dating, memories flood back that include: being stood up repeatedly, roofied, raped, hurt, abandoned, ghosted, lied to, cheated on, dismissed, and rejected. Friends tell me dating is a game. If that's the case, I'm clearly losing!

I can certainly tell how I'm doing emotionally by the men I attract. In my marriage, I barely drank at all, and newly single, it seemed I attracted alcoholics at the drop of a hat. It didn't make much sense because drinking wasn't all that important to me. Soon, though, a light bulb went on. I come from a long line of generational alcoholic abuse. See Chapter 2—Family Traditions for more details. Playing bartender was an honor to keep the liquid courage flowing. Alcoholism was an energy stuck in my field and blood line, even if I didn't know it. And, as with all energies, it was a mirror in my life. Whether we are aware of it or not, the energy we carry around, ours or someone else's, generally will attract more of the same.

There are many reasons we attract people into our lives that we do. Often, they fill a hole in our hearts. For example, why did I attract men who could barely afford to rent a room when I was living in a beautiful condo on the beach? Perhaps I needed to feel needed, safe, or superior. Coming from a divorce where I wasn't allowed to write in the checkbook, emailed schedules and was under a strict budget, I'm sure at the time there was fear stuck in me that goes something like, "If you have more than me you will try to control me."

And a huge shout out to the married men who have asked me out! Please, go home to your wives. Figure it out, or get divorced. For the love of God, don't bring someone else into your mess until you've been divorced for at least a year, preferably two, and have done inner work on yourself. I did go on a lovely date with a married man who told me he was single. About an hour into the date, he received a phone call, saying there was an emergency and ran out in a hurry. We set another date a week later. In the meantime, I found out he had gotten married three days before our date and was leaving on his honeymoon the very next day. About a month later, I ran into him and his new bride in line for a movie. It took everything in me to keep my mouth shut!

I've dated ages 29-67 years of age. Various nationalities, and homeless to millionaires. I've had close to 80 first dates, with only a handful of dates over the last five years. I met the 67-year-old in a doctor's office (I was 48 then). He invited me for a drink at a local bar. When I arrived, he said, "Wow, you are very sexy. Normally, I only date skinny women." Hmmm... I was taken aback and confused since he already knew what I looked like. I appreciated my size 12 curves and was giving him the benefit of the doubt, so I let the date continue. After a couple of hours, he said, "Will you do ecstasy and have sex?" Being the midwestern Christian girl I am, I honestly didn't know what ecstasy was other than a drug. I said, "Why do you need ecstasy to have sex?" He told me it would make him more empathetic towards me. Apparently, I was so out of his comfort zone of curves, he had to have drugs to see me naked! Goodness, gracious. Date over. And, yes, I spent the next hour googling ecstasy to find out what it was!

Here are a few more of my fun stories, for entertainment purposes only:

While on a first date, a man had his phone out most of the time, thumbing through his photos to show me the scantily dressed beautiful women he had dated in the past.

My boyfriend of a few months asked to borrow thousands of dollars. Repeatedly. And, when I blocked him on my phone, he borrowed his new girlfriend's phone to keep asking, while telling me how greedy I was because I wasn't sharing with him.

I sat down at packed bars half a dozen times, and within minutes there was no one else around. I know how to clear a room! Or someone would ask me regarding the empty seat next to me, "Is this seat taken"? I would say, "No, it's available." They literally would pick up the seat and take it to the other side of the bar! WOW! I must have been putting off some energy saying, get the F- away from me! What I was feeling, though, was rejected.

Whether it was an emotion stuck in my energy field, belonged to someone else, or a subconscious block, I knew it was unlikely that until I did more inner work around clearing it, I would keep attracting more of the same crazy.

And I think to myself, "What's wrong with me?"

I was vibrating loneliness. I was vibrating—I am lonely. Stay away from me. This is who I am at my core. What's stuck in there was everything I am. At the end of this chapter is a meditation to begin clearing the layers of stuck emotions, especially those in your spinal column.

The Merriam-Webster's Dictionary defines lonely as being without company. Desolate and sad from being alone. Cut off from others and producing a feeling of bleakness of desolation. My energy field must have been a shit show to attract the crazy characters that showed up at my door! Including, but not limited to: the homeless, alcoholic, narcissistic, drug addicted, possessive, back-stabbing, angry, lonely, seedy, needy, sociopathic, selfish, and obsessed. Need I go on? Although a work in progress myself, I knew there wasn't any way I was all that at once! I was also attracting others who subconsciously thought I could help.

Whether appreciated or not, I've always had a desire to be of help and service to others. In 3rd grade, I received an official award, "Eagerness to Help Others." When I asked my teacher what "eagerness" meant, however, the way she explained it made me feel it was a derogatory term insinuating that I was a bother to others. My "eagerness to help others" can be seen as intrusive. Although I meant well, others didn't often appreciate it, or frankly, even want it!

Many of the cray-cray men I was attracting finally disappeared when I shifted my belief honoring that everyone is on their individual journey and may not desire my help. I hung up my healing wand while I set my sights on a partner, not a project. I may see an easier way for someone, but my job isn't to fix people. My job is to accept others exactly where they are. I had to learn to allow others to be themselves, whether I agreed or not. It's their choice. It's not up to me to complete anyone or judge their journey. I've learned the hard way that they are only ready to hear the answer if they ask the question.

The world is set up to facilitate and accommodate the lives of partnered individuals. From legal and financial benefits to social norms and expectations, there are many structures in place that favor those who are in relationships. This can make it difficult for single individuals to navigate and participate fully in society. Most everything blesses the tandem pair. It's rare when two incomes are optional to buy a house and run a household. Until just recently, heterosexual married couples were the only couples who received tax benefits. Pairs are glamorized in Hollywood, while rom-coms flood the Hallmark channel with far-fetched romance stories.

Today's society still has a negative connotation surrounding being single. The idea that one must be partnered to be happy, fulfilled, or successful is deeply ingrained in our cultural psyche. This can lead to feelings of loneliness, isolation, and even shame for those not currently in a romantic relationship. There is a prevailing belief that single people are somehow unloved or unlovable. This stigma can lead to feelings of inadequacy and low self-worth, even for those who are perfectly content being single. Society often equates being in a relationship with being valued and loved, making it challenging for single individuals to feel accepted and appreciated.

However, being single is not inherently negative or undesirable. Being single has many benefits, including the freedom and flexibility to make decisions independently, the opportunity to focus on personal growth and self-care, and the ability to pursue one's interests and passions without compromise. And being single does not mean that one is unloved or unlovable. Love and connection can come from various sources, including friendships, family, and community. Romantic relationships are just one aspect of a fulfilling and meaningful life. A person doesn't need a life partner to feel the opposite of loneliness, which is connected and loved.

What's interesting to me is that although the number of unmarried Americans continues to grow, being single is still considered undesirable. One major factor contributing to the rise of unmarried Americans is the changing role of women in society. As women have gained greater access to education and career opportunities, they have become less reliant on marriage for financial security. This has led to more women delaying or choosing not to marry. Another contributing factor is the economic pressures faced by young adults. Living costs have increased significantly in recent years, making it more difficult for young people to afford traditional markers of adulthood, such as buying a home or starting a family. As a result, many are delaying marriage and focusing on building their careers and financial stability first.

There has also been a cultural shift in attitudes towards marriage and partnership. People increasingly value their independence and prioritize their needs and desires over societal expectations or norms. Many choose to remain single or live alone, enjoying the freedom and autonomy that comes with it. And regardless of the trends, challenges and stigmas are still associated with being unmarried or living alone.

For example, unmarried individuals may face workplace or social discrimination, and there may be negative stereotypes about people who choose to live alone. Whether one chooses to marry, live with a partner, or remain single and independent, what matters most is the ability to live a fulfilling and meaningful life on one's own terms.

Numerous times in my travels around the globe, I am surrounded by happy, smiling couples. Hotels are full of lovers holding hands and laying poolside, kissing. I feel out of place. I look around and notice all the couples and families traveling together.

And I ask myself the question,

What's wrong with me?

What did I do to deserve this aloneness?

One of my sons nonchalantly informed me that my value as a woman decreases with age, and men's value increases with age. I was left speechless at that moment. As much as I disagree with his statement, sadly, I believe much of the world thinks the same.

And I ask myself again,

What's wrong with me?

What did I do to deserve this aloneness?

Recently feeling unseen, I asked to see my own dating energy in meditation. I placed all the energy regarding men, dating, and my soul-dating wounds into a love bubble and asked to see what was happening. To begin, I just wanted to observe. What I saw answered many questions about why I was pushing men away. I saw myself walking into a deep dark ocean full of sharks swimming in a circle around me, eager to hurt me. They were hungry, angry sharks. This was a confirmation of my feelings toward dating at the time. I dip my toe in the ocean of men only to get it bitten off.

To change the energy of my dating life, I began to speak light language and love into the bubble I created in meditation. It took quite a while. Typically, energy moves faster! It would shift, then go right back. It did that a few times. I continued to pour love and light into it while setting the intention for the highest and best for all involved.

The energy finally began to shift permanently. The water ocean drained. The sharks turned into men—all different sizes and shapes. Different professions, clothes. And focuses with one thing in common—all with hurt little boys inside of them. I saw their hurt souls. I saw their eagerness to partner with a woman of substance, A woman who saw them and loved them for who they were.

As I asked for men with high values, conscious, awake, and self-aware to step forward, my pool of men got much thinner. I was able to walk among them. I wasn't afraid of them like before. I could walk up to them and shake their hand (which I thought was funny). I could allow them to be who they are as I stood in my power, getting to know them without taking on their energy. It felt empowering and exciting. Almost easy. I saw them for who they were.

I've heard it said that relationships are where people work out their issues from the past. I must have had a ton of issues! And, while shocking, at the very least, they collectively and individually taught me something about myself. I learned how to communicate in a non-reactive way. They taught me to love myself first and be true to myself—no matter what. I'm ever thankful for the opportunity to grow as a woman, realizing that I do not need to settle. I believe women shouldn't sit back and allow men (and vice versa) to take advantage of or be treated with such disdain. We live in a day and age that calls for broader respect, honest communication, and deeper intimacy. Nothing less should be accepted.

I invite both sexes always to be honest with their date. First, though, you must be honest with yourself. Why are you really dating? If it's only for the thrill of a few moments of pleasure, make sure those expectations are expressed upfront. What are your underlying intentions? Mis-communicated or non-spoken expectations will leave your date wondering what hit him/her when they thought they were building an emotional relationship and you just wanted a physical one. Deep communication—open, honest, and deliberate—is the key to dating and harvesting a relationship that lasts.

Regardless, the world is our mirror, reflecting to us what we project onto it. In the context of relationships, this means that the people we attract into our lives and the dynamics that play out in our interactions with them directly reflect our inner state.

At first glance, this idea can be hard to swallow. It can be easy to think that the problems we experience in our relationships are caused by other people's behavior or external circumstances beyond our control. However, looking deeper, we often find that our inner state and beliefs are at the root of these issues. For example, if we need help with trust issues, we may find ourselves constantly attracting partners who are unfaithful or unreliable. If we fear abandonment, we may unconsciously push people away or cling to them in unhealthy ways. If we struggle with feelings of unworthiness, we may find ourselves in relationships where we are not valued or respected.

This is not to say that we are solely responsible for the behavior of others or that we should blame ourselves for every relationship difficulty we encounter. However, we have a choice in how we show up in our relationships, and by taking responsibility for our thoughts, feelings, and behaviors, we can create healthier, more fulfilling connections with others.

Increasing our self-awareness and understanding of our values and inner motives will create a strong relationship foundation. Once we better understand our inner landscape, we can begin to make conscious choices about how we interact with others. For example, if we notice that we are critical or judgmental, we can work on cultivating a more compassionate and accepting mindset. If we struggle with setting boundaries, we can practice asserting ourselves in a healthy way.

Ultimately, the world is our reflection in relationships, because the way we show up in our interactions with others reflects our own inner state. We can create healthier and more fulfilling connections with others by taking responsibility for our thoughts, feelings, and behaviors.

I could tell how I was really doing by the relationships and circumstances I was attracting. Often it wasn't pretty! For the difficult ones, I would evaluate each one, wondering WHY I attracted that person/event into my life. One more time around the roundabout of loneliness, recognizing I'm being given a gift of time to love myself unconditionally and heal deep wounds. It's a gift to me, who has spent decades caring for everyone else. I began to feel these feelings to process them and stop pushing them away. In allowing them just to be... my inner being could relax, and I slowly began to feel safe and secure on my own.

And, then, the roundabouts get further and further from each other. The triggers lessen. The hole in my heart begins to fill. Soon, I can talk more about being alone without tears falling. I am comfortable with myself now. Being alone has allowed me time to regain confidence while strengthening my broken spirit.

You may ask me, why on earth do I even consider getting back in the ring of dating? I still believe in marriage, partnering, and people. After many failed attempts of dating and finding solace in the world, I am settled into myself, whether single or partnered. I know my worth as a woman, and it's not tied to whether I have a shiny diamond on my ring finger. What I came to embrace is that because I am alone doesn't mean I have to be lonely.

And, although my journey began with self-defeating questions, inviting in more self-deprecating answers, my guidance led me out of that rabbit hole into a higher perspective of this journey. My entire life has changed by shifting the questions in my mind and focusing on what I want to bring into my life (instead of what I do not want). It's all in the new question I ask myself from a higher perspective that will lead me to the destination of my desire.

The Wisdom Within

Now It's Your Turn!

Scan the QR Code below to hear Lara guide you through a deep light language meditation to clear loneliness. Have a pen and paper ready to journal your thoughts.

Scan me

14

Everything is Energy

So what if I was to tell you that not only is everything energy
It is a virtual reality, there's a hologram, that is kind
of the matrix
Because everything is energy
And that energy is everywhere

~Envine

AI Demon Midget Removal ° Gargoyle and Mothman removal ° Psychic dagger removal from back and neck ~mostly from an unidentified, cowardly male ° Snakes and shit ° Black spider web removal ° Dump portal sanitation ° Furry animal with claws in neck removal ° Sentient blob removal/ hazmat ° Homing Device

Those Venmo payment descriptions above are from a client. This particular lightworker is a target for the darkest of the dark, yet continues to shine his light. I'm honored that I can support him on his journey to hold the light.

I quickly learned that energy was everything when I was deep in healing mode about ten years ago. Feeling stuffed full like a Thanksgiving turkey, others' energy and emotions, as well as my own, overtook my body. Even so, my aura was wide-open, allowing more unwelcome energies to make their home in my field. Daily, my priority became clearing my energy.

In Chapter 6—Learning to Fly, I write about being a highly sensitive empathic. I've had to own my energy field. I'm responsible for what's in my field and what I'm putting into the world. Without mastering myself and my energy, I am left to collect whatever is in the collective consciousness, and no doubt its energies want to dumb me down. One of the primary shifts I made was to stop telling myself every day, "I'm so sensitive; I feel everyone's everything." Whatever we focus on, we expand. Instead, I remind myself daily, "I am strong, healthy, and in my power."

Nikola Tesla says, "If you want to find the secrets of the universe, think in terms of energy, frequency, and vibration." Over the years of studying this invisible world, I began seeing the power in these unseen and intangible concepts. This invisible force is so strong that it shifts reality. Yet the visual proof of it, actually seeing it with our eyes, is elusive. How do you explain that which you can't see? How do you master the invisible? It starts with a knowing. It starts with knowing it's there in the first place.

Think back to 10th grade science class. You'll recall that everything in the universe is made of energy. EVERYTHING IS ENERGY. Physical atoms are made up of vortices of energy that are constantly spinning and vibrating. This invisible energy is present all of the time, despite the fact that our human eye can't see it. We are all these energy bubbles walking around, spanning about an arm's length. We are spirits in a physical body with an energy field that outlines our body called an aura. This auric field can be read by scientific devices, and is proven to exist and change depending on what's happening in your environment. The secrets to having happy relationships, making great decisions, financial stress or success, vibrant health, and much more are within your energy field or your bubble.

For example, have you ever wondered how when you walk into a room full of people, you always end up talking to the right person, the right people, and avoiding those who don't feel right to you? You are intuitively feeling energy. Your spidey-senses draw you to like-minded, familiar energy—energy that resonates with yours. Often though, what happens is our energy bubbles clash with others. When this happens, our energies aren't matching. They're not vibrating at the same frequency as two magnets repelling each other. And, for highly sensitive empaths, a third phenomenon happens as well. You may draw others' energy and emotions into yourself, causing you to download what you resonate with most. Immediately you can feel their pain or sadness as your own.

Often our fields get damaged in life. Stress, divorce, trauma, bullying, gossip, surgeries, alcohol, and even crowds, can cause our energetic field, our bubbles, to weaken. This is where it gets fascinating. All of this combined with years of stuck energy, old emotions, and trauma, our bodies start to become overwhelmed. They can feel jammed with dense, heavy energy. And as I mentioned, some of this stuck energy and emotions we're holding aren't ours.

Life's daily pressures and circumstances have many folks feeling overwhelmed and stressed to the max. This relentless pressure is causing addiction issues and emotional and physical pain. Staying in this stressful state can create health issues or feelings of being stuck in life or business. A decline in creativity, clarity, and productivity can also occur if the energy is allowed to continue. Making good decisions goes out the door, too! And again, regardless of where this energy came from, this overwhelming energy, this stress energy, or who it belongs to, if it ends up in your field, you're responsible for it.

We are each responsible for owning our energy—no matter where it came from. If you don't like how you feel, your life, or your business, it's up to you to shift it. What's happening outside almost always reflects what is happening within us. Not always, but as a general rule. To change our surroundings, we must look within and work our way out to our energy field.

All of the unique tools and techniques that I practice on clients, I first practiced on myself. Little by little, day by day, I began to heal those gaping wounds that were bleeding out. Things I had struggled with all my life began to fall away. All because I took time each day to clear my energy field of stuck emotions, examine old beliefs, and pour the highest vibration of divine light into myself – mainly utilizing light language. Finally, I could keep my aura sealed and chakras cleared and balanced while transmuting the extra unnecessary energies my body was holding. Then and only then did I venture into helping others.

I've had clients tell me they felt like they had a chiropractic adjustment without ever touching them. Others say they felt roto-rooted. And others even said they felt nothing! Most come to me with concerns about relationship issues, money, or health challenges. Others have more specific needs, like the client above. Although I giggle when I read his summary of what I've cleared, it's no laughing matter when these energies take you down—sometimes for weeks.

In individual sessions with people over the years, I've seen it all—then something new comes along. I've worked with all ages—0 to 98. Each session is unique, and each person needs something entirely different. I tune into the energy field and then go in layer by layer, chakra by chakra, down the spine, into organs, and then deeper into their Akashic records and generational lineage.

An initial session includes the following:

> moving stuck energy and emotions
> relieving stress and pain
> activating your unlimited potential
> clearing and balancing chakras
> imprinting healing and regenerating codes
> repairing holes and tears in auric fields
> imprinting a higher vibration into cells
> recalibrating the body and energy field
> releasing Discordant Energies (entities)

In additional sessions, we can dive deeper into topics such as:

> return soul fragments
> implants and trackers deactivated and removed
> de-cording from past loves, homes, work, and circumstances
> de-cording from excessive alcohol, sugar, and other addictions
> de-cording from others who are siphoning energy
> disable and remove energetic interference and negative influences
> remove distraction, distortion, and interference energy
> remove physical and energetic parasites/worms
> calming and clearing your nervous system
> remove walk-in spirits and over-souls
> resetting your body back to love
> dissolving and removal of degenerative energies and embedded blockages
> collective, Individual, and Generational trauma

shadow elements
rape energies
numerous types of implants
false light frequencies
holographic inserts
phantom and false matrices
disconnected mind synapsis
energetic parasites
AI spiders

An energy session can also release energetic interference/attack by negative influences—spirits, frequencies, technology, contracts, vows, oaths, spells, pacts, bindings, or agreements. In addition to removing the negative energies, I instruct divine teams to correct, repair, and reinstall the person's highest divine blueprint. Their energy field is refilled with love and light.

Chapter 8 includes a detailed explanation of home and land clearings. In this chapter, you may be as fascinated as I am to write about energy clearing in people, things, and nonphysical items. Everything is living energy and holds energy. 3-D tangible objects like people, homes, land, spaces, brick-and-mortar business, china, or furniture all vibrate at a specific frequency, while having the potential to be infected with different unseen energies. Nonphysical entities like an online business, websites, or social media also hold energy and can potentially be contaminated with distorted energies.

Physical Items

For several years, I've intuitively heard it's time to give away my Christmas Spode china. I have 12 full place settings, plus many other extras. Since I was a little girl, my parents and other loved ones would give me a set each year plus accessories. Instead of dolls, I relished collecting my china, filling my hope chest.

Everything is Energy

I had just returned from a family trip to Indiana when I kept hearing in my inner psyche, "Spode." My Spode was pinging me for attention. I knew it had a message for me, yet I rather wanted to ignore it! I loved my Spode, but it was beginning to feel very heavy.

What is pinging in your soul? What is pinging in your body? It's attempting to get a message to you. What do you keep hearing or seeing repeatedly and haven't done anything about? We don't know what we don't know. I went back to the basics to uncover what was happening with my Spode.

1. Be Still.
2. Silence the mind chatter.
3. Meditating on what it wants to tell us.

Reluctantly, I began to tune in. I asked the Spode what it wanted to say. It didn't say anything. Next, I called up the energy of it. It was five stories high! I was so surprised at the hugeness. No wonder I was feeling it so strongly. I saw the energy of each person who had eaten off it, made it, and given it to me. I saw the memory attached to each piece as well. I would get it out the day after Thanksgiving and use it until the New Year. I saw and felt all of the memories tied to this particular china. It represented a time in my life when I felt loved and surrounded by family. Feeling like I had sacrificed enough of my physical belongings in my many moves, I had zero intention of giving it up.

Spode china wasn't exactly on my adult boys' list of items desired. I continued to hold onto it for dear life because I knew that as I let it go, I would be saying goodbye forever to a particularly happy time in my life. The time when I was a housewife, mom, pillar of the community, and member of a large church community. Now, only crumbs of that time are left, with the rest lying crumbled on the ground.

After the session I did with myself and the Spode to uncover what was happening, I felt much lighter and clear-headed. Before my next move, I kept some pieces for myself and packaged all of the Spode for my sister and nieces in Indiana. I was thrilled knowing it was on its way to being appreciated and utilized.

My Christmas china is only one example of an item that may need energy cleared. Photos, jewelry, artwork, vases, electronics, furniture (especially antiques), and anything physical also holds living energy. If your energy is off somehow, it could be tied to something as simple as clearing the energy on your favorite vintage coffee cup!

Nonphysical Items

As I was facilitating energy sessions on people, land, homes, businesses, and their material items, I began to see that I could also apply my unique techniques to intangible, nonphysical materials. For example, an online business that delivers a service or a specific social media channel.

We can also apply these tools to a person's money story. In any of these cases, we take all of the components that make up the intangible item. The clearing would include the energy of their money mistakes, bank accounts, investment accounts, generational imprints, subconscious beliefs about money, and fear or guilt around having money. Anything related to their money beliefs, imprints, or thoughts would be included. In meditation, all of these are put in a bubble of love for the clearing and healing of a person's money story to allow for more abundance and wealth. Before the clearing, we intuit information that we need to know, allow for the clearing, and then fill the money story bubble of energy back up with divine love. Lastly, it's imperative that your energy is in alignment with receiving the abundance. Your money story, although unseen, tells an energetic story.

The implications of healing are endless, with the power to shift the energy of the physical and non-physical. In addition to money, health, relationships, career, websites, and more are all available for transformation. It's powerful to invite the story to come alive for healing.

Working from Home

Working from home (WFH) is ripe with perks; however, it has created numerous challenges never experienced before. One of the unique issues that you may be experiencing is a heavy, overwhelming feeling in your office or throughout your home. All walls, spaces, homes, and land retain living energy like people and businesses. Everything—matter or non-matter – holds memories and thought forms.

For example, let's say you are on Zoom business calls most of the day. The numerous folks you connect to (even through the computer) are all expelling energy into your energy field and home. In the past, when you went to an office, it was easier to keep work stress at the office. That is no longer the case. Other people's energy, including; heated conversations, anger, frustration, and stress, are all piling up in your home. You may experience it as you sit at your desk with an overwhelming, heavy feeling. You may also begin to feel confused or stuck yourself.

Floating Thought Forms

We are receivers of thought forms. Dr. Bruce Lipton explains, "The mind is energy. When you think, you transmit energy, and thoughts are more powerful than chemistry." Everyone, at all times, is releasing their thoughts and emotions unbeknownst to themselves. Sadly, most thoughts floating around the collective consciousness aren't positive and empowering.

Twice recently, walking into the grocery, I have strolled into what I call a dark blob energy thought form. How's that for the fancy descriptive label from a professional? These are highly concentrated balls of collective energy featuring negative thoughts and low-vibration energy of anger, frustration, and more. I know it IMMEDIATELY as soon as I'm in it. I'll be joyfully walking along, and all of a sudden, even though the sidewalk looks clear and no one is around, I walk right into this goo of dark gunk. Before I know it, within minutes, I become a raving bitch, uncertain which way is up, confused, and disoriented. I begin to have immediate negative thoughts. And all this before I even entered the grocery stores! It feels a bit like getting energetically slimed, yet invisible to the naked eye. When this occurs, energy work has been the only solution to clear this immediately.

Energy cannot be created or destroyed; however, it can be transmuted —- as in changed from one form of energy to another or moved from one location to another. As people release their energies that no longer serve them, if they do not specify where it goes, it will jump onto the next closest object that will hold it or float until someone walks into it to pick it up.

It's always up to us to own our energy and control our thoughts. Although that energy I walked through wasn't technically mine, most likely, there was something in me for it to attach to. I am responsible for recognizing the energy shift and doing something about it. You may think about all the times that you 'all of a sudden' felt off or got triggered. This is the daily work. SLOW DOWN, take a breath, and connect with yourself.

The profound understanding that everything is energy, and the ability to observe and shift it, brings about a transformative perspective on our existence. Energy, in its various forms, is a fundamental force that flows through all aspects of life. As we recognize that energy can never truly be destroyed but instead transmuted, we are empowered to harness its potential for positive change. Through focused and intentional practices like prayer, we possess the capacity to transmute heavy energies into love, leading to a profound sense of well-being and a radiant aura of light. This knowledge transcends physical boundaries, allowing us to clear and cleanse spaces, objects, and even digital realms with love and respect. Embracing this power to shift energy brings harmony and a sense of interconnectedness with the universe, leaving us enriched by the boundless possibilities of love's transformative influence.

> An LA integrative wellness coach and her husband, a psychologist, both work from home full-time. She writes, "Along with my own clients' emotional issues in my office, my husband's clients are progressively struggling with higher rates of anxiety and depression, and it's all coming into our bedroom where he works. I started experiencing dark spiritual attacks while I was sleeping, then the lightbulb went on as to what was happening. I called Lara immediately! After her clearing, I can SLEEP, and my home/office feels much lighter. I have more energy and a clearer focus. Work continues to flow in just at the right amount. HUGE energy shift for us! It is profoundly and powerfully affected my sense of peace and well-being."

Jennifer was struggling with grief and sadness from some loved ones who passed away years ago. She was having trouble with the kids and struggling to lead a balanced life. It was work, work, work. Money was coming in very slowly. She was over-volunteering. She had a beautiful home, husband, and family from the outside looking in, but she felt like her life was stuck and heavy. She came to me for help with all of this. We did coaching to incorporate these spiritual practices that I am revealing today. We did energy work with her and her husband, with her two teenage kids, and a house clearing as well. Everything holds energy. You have to look at all of it. When I'm working with a client, we look at not just you and your field, but we look at your family. We look at your house, car, animals, all of it. So the energy work gives you a head start, and the light language is how I do my energy work. It gives you a head start to support you while you look within to master your energy.

Now, how do things look in their life? Business for both of them is working very well. Her husband's business... He would invoice people and they wouldn't pay and now people are paying on time, if not early. Their house feels great. She was able to redecorate and really deal with the grief that she was feeling when her loved ones passed. All of that through the work that we did.

Debbie is a physician, mom, wife, and spiritually connected. She wanted more meaning in her work and needed help balancing all the balls in her life, home, career, kids, health, and relationships while she was growing spiritually. After a year of spiritual coaching, clearing energy, deepening her already present meditation practice, and working through triggers, she was able to create deeper connections with her loved ones. Debbie says, "Through working with Lara, I was able to reconnect to myself and Spirit which helped me in every area of my life. My heart and soul feel deeply nourished and I feel more meaning at my same place of work. Her work has helped me recognize and reorganize my life priorities based off my own values. There is an inner peace now that flows me I never had before."

Sarah came to me, struggling to get her healing business going. She knows that her business is a reflection of her own energy. And she knew she needed to do the inside job of clearing away all that stuck energy. It was holding her back from her own potential, her own greatness. We uncovered the blocks that were holding her back through our coaching work together. She raised her vibration, expanded her consciousness, and she was able to perfectly align to her own true soul purpose. And for her, it was based in the mind chatter, the old story of, "I'm not good enough." Today she is rocking her business with a steady flow of income, loving that her business is so meaningful to her, and it is in line with who she is.

> Julie and her family were struggling. There was fighting in the house with a lot of company coming in/out. As a mom of three small kids, she felt like she had lost herself. Julie didn't know who she was or what she wanted anymore. There was also stealing at her husband's business. After consistent coaching, a house clearing, a business clearing, sessions with her husband and children, the entire family has a whole new outlook on life. Julie says, "Lara gave us a new toolbox to reset our entire life. Our whole family has grown spiritually and vibrationally. We have a deep peace and sleep well at night. Clarity returned. Money started flowing again. And, most importantly, we are enjoying life together again."

Below are a few examples of word for word Intuitive sessions:

Jenna's House/Space:

As I tune into the space, here are the words that come up— stressful, full. I'm having trouble breathing as I remotely walk around. Chaotic energy, whether there is a lot of stuff or not. I feel like there is plenty of room, although it's FULL. This FULL feeling is being reflected in your business and your body as well... meaning that there is no more room for additional clients. No room for a man/connection/friends. No room/ no time to let anything else in. I'm seeing a knock at the door and energetically, your back is to the door as you are sucked into your portal of work and can't hear the knock. It's more opportunities, more clients, more money, friends, a lover etc. It's all there—but outside your door. There is no room for the door to open and something else to walk in to hang out with you.

I'm feeling like there is a deep belief that you deserve this aloneness. That you did something wrong or feel guilty. LET THAT GO. This is the life you get organized, decluttered, de-stressed, let the old stuff go that no longer serves you, while you learn to lean into and manifest the life of your dreams. Before you can DREAM it, though, you have to start weeding through the field of your life and house/space in order to find that new dream that is buried. Once you can connect to that DREAM that is buried, you'll be able to open the door to allow it in. Right now, though, even if you knew what it was, it wouldn't be able to get through the door.

For now, I've put your house in a bubble of love and am clearing anything that isn't love, joy, peace or gratitude. Your guides are showing me within 7-10 days as your personal energy session is taking effect, you will be able to think clearer about what you want to shift in your house to make room for the new. It all works together—as you shift yourself, your house/space HAS to shift, as does your business!

Avery, Age 23

He's very kind and tender. Has a huge heart. He has an open energy field with few energy boundaries. Sponge-Bob, where he soaks up others emotions/thoughts/feelings quickly before he even knows it. His quick angry reactions are part of this response to holding others' stuff.

I do not see damage from his concussion. What I do see is

that within a day or two after the fall, he was infiltrated with a dark energy. The concussion opened him up and made him more susceptible to receiving this darker energy. This is not who Avery is, so this different energy in him caused him to act out in ways that were uncharacteristic for him, hence the unusual outbursts, not sleeping, anxiety, etc. I'm told that the energy that infiltrated him was responsible for 90% or more of how he's been feeling/acting differently. I can see him within a couple of weeks (if not sooner) with a new, happier stance and more energy. I see him laughing and joking and being more himself. Quite the successful man, in life, business, and love!

Eddie, Age 22

Relationships with others are #1 to him—even over his own self-care. He doesn't think he's worthy. Feels less than his brother. This is a karmic lesson between them. HUGE heart and very sensitive, as well. He is an old soul, galactic energy. He has great power and on occasion he will feel it and it scares him so he shuts himself down even more. In the past, this power got him killed, so he's keeping himself small right now. What's holding him back from being his best self is only his own subconscious fear of success, and what I see is almost superhero-like power in him. He lives vicariously through theatre but especially video games. I see open portals in his room from the video games. Shutting those now during this session.

I cleared some karmic energy between the two brothers that was holding them back from being their best.

I do not see any dark energy of any kind. However, his energy field is dense and heavy. Hard to describe but what I'm being shown is as he has played over the years—games, watches tv, etc.—other peoples' energies and dumbed-down programs/energies have become one with his. The more he "plays" or the tv/computer is on, the energetically heavier he gets. This heaviness doesn't allow him to feel his own stuff (which is the purpose and what he wants), hence he isn't motivated. It's literally keeping him stuck. He also had a negative thought form that had taken over his mind.

Now It's Your Turn!

Scan the QR Code below to hear Lara guide you through a light language meditation for a deep energy clearing. Have a pen and paper ready to journal your thoughts.

Scan me

15

Unwritten

I am unwritten
Can't read my mind
I'm undefined
I'm just beginning
The pen's in my hand
Ending unplanned

I break tradition
Sometimes my tries are outside the lines
We've been conditioned to not make mistakes
But I can't live that way

Release your inhibitions
Feel the rain on your skin
No one else can feel it for you
Only you can let it in
No one else, no one else
Can speak the words on your lips
Drench yourself in words unspoken
Live your life with arms wide open

~Natasha Bedingfield

Recently, I sensed the all-too-familiar shadows of depression settling in. Loneliness and health struggles seemed to overtake my every step. Transitioning to another new city, aiming to establish roots, make friends, and find community and healthcare support proved to be a more daunting task than I had envisioned. Asking for help during overwhelming moments can be a formidable challenge. Just as a drowning person finds it hard to call out for help, a person in the grip of depression also grapples with reaching out. And navigating life's trials alone only amplifies the sense of isolation.

Having experienced various degrees of depression over the years, I recognize the signals as it creeps in. My depressive state deepens when a relentless tide of pent-up anger and frustration turns inward. The ceaseless weariness of constant relocation and new beginnings has taken its toll. The unending pressure to build a sustainable business while balancing unseen energy forces has drained me. Confronting multiple autoimmune ailments and other health hurdles daily has nurtured frustration that has morphed into anger. And facing all this solo for the past decade has bred a growing resentment within me.

And yet, I understand that I am the steward of my energy and the magnet for what comes into my life.

Despite the gloomy cloud hanging over this year, and despite being far from my family, I planned a special birthday retreat—a celebration unwinding at a nearby Ritz Carlton on the shoreline. Even though my friend had to cancel last-minute due to an emergency, I resolved to proceed with my plans, even if it meant going alone. Upon reaching the hotel and parking by the valet station, I remained unnoticed amidst the flurry of cars. This continued for nearly fifteen minutes. With no assistance in sight, I chose to depart. Unsure of my next move, I pondered whether to rejoin the queue or head back home.

Disappointment and invisibility weighed heavily as I drove back, calmly calling the hotel's General Manager to cancel my reservation without penalty. Amidst the chaotic traffic, accompanied by classical tunes, I questioned the energy I might have projected to become so overlooked. Intrigued by why the attendants didn't notice me, I wondered about the energy I emitted. What did they perceive from their vantage point?

As I pulled into my driveway, I realized I likely went unnoticed due to my status as a single woman sitting alone in a car, probably making a delivery or awaiting someone. After all, what solo woman checks into a Ritz alone? Well, that would be me, on my birthday. Solo travel has been my norm. It wasn't the first time my singularity posed an issue while traveling, but it was the first time I was blatantly overlooked.

Acknowledging the need to strike a balance between engaging with the world and remaining impervious to its energies, there's always inner work to be done. My energy field appears to polarize—repelling or magnetizing people. Despite the ongoing challenges, my commitment remains unwavering to navigate life more consciously. I persistently pursue personal growth and a deeper understanding of both myself and the energies enveloping me.

Although I woke up in my own bed, my birthday dawned with a different atmosphere than anticipated. A sense of melancholy threatened to engulf me. Ordinarily, I would have secluded myself indoors all weekend, discouraged over my solitude after the hotel incident. But on this birthday, I chose a different way.

Aware of my power to shape my energy and attraction, I walked along the beach, clearing my thoughts and conversing with my boys on the phone. Spontaneously, I booked a whale-watching boat tour for the following day. This allowed me to rise above the turmoil, observing the circumstances without descending further. I intentionally refused to pity myself for being alone on my birthday, yet again. Nor did I wish to spend the day watching Netflix for hours on end. Instead, I sought what would make my heart sing (whale watching), shifting my thoughts and energy. It was a simple act of stepping out of my comfort zone, choosing to immerse myself fully in the present.

Distinguishing between clinical depression requiring medication and teetering on the edge of a depressive state, I found myself in the latter category this time. I harnessed my mental prowess to redirect my energy and thoughts, forging a new memory. Detecting the onset of sadness before it snowballs into depression became my strategy to pivot toward a more joyful state.

I've drawn an invisible line in the sand, embracing a fresh approach. Self-compassion, self-awareness, and rewiring my thoughts are my chosen tools for crafting a new life. Unless I'm genuinely clinically depressed, external circumstances needn't dominate my inner world. I possess the ability to practice introspection and reset. Just as your life's narrative rests within your grasp, mine is within me. Guided by faith and trust, I opt for a co-creative venture with Spirit, welcoming the boundless possibilities on the horizon.

Individually, we're all being invited to embrace a consistent spiritual practice, heighten self-awareness, and reshape our negative thoughts. These tumultuous times we inhabit necessitate an enhanced understanding of our internal landscapes, particularly in relation to the broader collective.

This collection of chapters serves as an invitation to embark on a lifelong journey of self-discovery and empowerment. We have witnessed the power of family, intuition, and words; we have navigated the labyrinth of our minds and embraced change and vulnerability. We have learned that life is about finding the courage to soar amid challenges, to cherish our homes and relationships, and to dance with our shadows. As we continue forward, let us carry the wisdom of these chapters in our hearts, drawing from them the strength to face our demons, the humility to accept our imperfections, and the compassion to connect with our fellow travelers. For in the tapestry of life, we are but a thread, intricately woven with others, and together, we create a masterpiece of love and understanding.

I pray that my personal stories, practical guidance, and insightful wisdom was of help to you to unlock your inner potential and find greater meaning and security within yourself. Each subsequent chapter delves into a unique aspect of this journey, offering insights and practical advice for you to tap into your inner guidance and create a more fulfilling life. Keep embracing introspection, nurturing empathy, and weaving a world woven with threads of love, compassion, and connection. With a sense of wonder and awe, we step into the unknown, eager to shape our narratives with purpose and love.

Chapter 1-Walking Alone painted a poignant picture of the impact of emotions on an unborn child's development, revealing the significance of emotions in shaping our lives.

Chapter 2-Family Traditions explored the inherited patterns and behaviors that influence our choices and relationships, inviting you to reflect on your own family dynamics.

Chapter 3-She Talks to Angels taught us the power of intuition and spirituality, urging us to listen to the subtle whispers of our souls and trust our inner guidance. Through this profound connection to the spiritual realm, we discover a deeper sense of purpose and meaning in life.

In recognizing the potency of our words, ***Chapter 4-Words are Energy*** encouraged us to be mindful of the language we use. Our words hold the power to uplift or destroy, to heal or harm. By harnessing the positive energy of language, we can create a more compassionate and harmonious world.

In the intricate realm of the mind, **Chapter 5-Mind Games** warns us of the self-imposed limitations and illusions that hinder our growth. We learn that true liberation lies in mastering our thoughts and transforming negative patterns into empowering ones.

Chapter 6-Learning to Fly inspires you to step out of your comfort zone and manage energy sensitivity as a master.

Chapter 7-Time to Move On acknowledged that change is an inherent part of life as we learn the art of letting go. By gracefully bidding farewell to what no longer serves us, we create space for new beginnings and opportunities to manifest. Portal keeping and land healing are welcomed from the Universe.

Chapter 8- Our House explored the connection between our physical environment and our well-being, encouraging you to create spaces that nurture your inner selves. The warmth and security of our houses serve as a sanctuary, nurturing our spirits and fostering a harmonious environment of love and acceptance.

Chapter 9-Dancing with Your Shadows speaks of embracing our imperfections and vulnerabilities. As we come to terms with our shadow selves, we unlock the power of self-acceptance, leading us on a path of authenticity and self-discovery.

Chapter 10-Just Be Held assures us that we are not alone in our struggles, especially as we encounter Dark Nights of the Soul. We are cradled by the loving embrace of the Universe, and it is okay to lean on others for support during challenging times.

Chapter 11-Jumping Timelines introduced us to the concept of infinite possibilities and parallel realities. Each decision we make creates a unique path, and by being conscious of our choices, we can shape a destiny aligned with our highest aspirations.

Through the prism of **Chapter 12-Sweet Emotions,** we recognized the beauty of human emotions and the richness they bring to life. Emotions are a canvas of our experiences, enabling us to connect with others on a profound level. They are meant to be felt, not numbed.

Chapter 13-Lonely People examined the impact of loneliness on our well-being, offering strategies for building meaningful connections.

As we delved into the profound understanding that **Everything is Energy** in Chapter 14, we grasp the interconnection between all living things. By recognizing our energetic ties to the universe, we become mindful of our actions and the impact they have on the greater whole. This chapter brings the book full circle, reinforcing the idea that our thoughts, emotions, and actions shape our reality.

The Wisdom Within: Cracking the Secrets of Meaning, Purpose, & Security has illuminated the path to crafting a higher vibrational existence through collaboration with Spirit—a journey that necessitates dismantling outdated constructs. The life we clung to in the rearview mirror must yield to the process of transformation, allowing for the emergence of a fortified foundation of self-love and joy. Shedding the remnants of obsolete beliefs and patterns can be a trying and emotional endeavor. Throughout this book, I have given you unique tools and techniques to crack the secrets of meaning, purpose, and security. If you did before, no longer will you find these essential pieces outside of yourself. What used to work no longer works. Only when we go within navigating the unpredictable and often rocky landscape will we feel secure no matter what is going on in the chaotic world. Know that you can rise above the drama at any time during your day by checking in with yourself. Allow the quiet to calm your soul while you release that which you longer need. As you've likely come to discover within the pages of this book:

The way OUT of chaos is IN.

The way OUT of disconnection is IN.

The way OUT of numbing yourself is IN.

The key to unlocking a life characterized by flow, equilibrium, and harmony lies in authentic self-embrace and introspection. This entails confronting the neglected facets of our being—the ones we pushed aside when they sought to communicate with us. It's about acknowledging the self that yearned for attention, even if it resorted to inciting discomfort within our bodies. It's the self we've often been hesitant to confront in the mirror. *The Wisdom Within: Cracking the Secrets of Meaning, Purpose, & Security* beckons us to traverse a spectrum of tools, from surface-level kayaking to profound deep-sea diving into our psyche. In a world undergoing profound transformation, we're summoned to explore our inner realms. Amidst the turbulence of change, take solace in the reassurance that life persists on the other side. Embrace this transformative journey, shedding the outdated to pave the way for renewal. Amidst the collapse of structures, find solace in the grounding of self.

During my impromptu whale-watching adventure, I was fortunate to witness the majestic presence of four awe-inspiring blue whales, the Earth's largest creatures. The experience of gracefully gliding across the ocean's expanse aboard a swiftly navigating vessel brought about a rejuvenation of my energy, elevating my frequency to unprecedented levels. No matter how the day commences, we possess the power to shape its conclusion according to our own choices.

May we embrace the future chapters of our lives with open arms, knowing that the journey is not about reaching a destination, but about savoring the beauty of every step along the way. As we walk this path, hand in hand with the Universe, may we find solace in the knowledge that we are, and always will be, an integral part of the grand tapestry of existence. With the story's ending still unwritten, the pen is in your hand.

What's Next?

Although our time together has come to a close, there remains a vast expanse of self-discovery awaiting those who embark on a lifelong journey inward. I extend an invitation to utilize this as your guiding compass, whether you are starting afresh or delving deeper into your inner realm. Understand that beneath the layers of what you wish to shed, you are already whole and healed.

Similar to the gradual peeling of an onion, we shed what no longer serves us, day by day, bit by bit, slowly revealing more of our authentic selves. There's no need to rush; this isn't a competition. Life is meant to be savored slowly and with intention. It is in those daily moments of pause that the true journey unfolds. If you would like additional support with your inward exploration, please visit me at, LaraJaye.com.

About the Author

Lara Jaye is an international spiritual life coach, intuitive consultant, best-selling author, captivating speaker, podcast host, energy healer and a Light Language pioneer. Her work is focused on reshaping the paradigm of life and business success with her unique blend of spiritual wisdom and insightful guidance. Lara leverages her deep understanding of the human psyche and a remarkable ability to tap into the higher consciousness of clients to unlock their utmost potential in both their professional endeavors and personal lives. She is passionate about guiding others inward to foster a more joyful, meaningful, and purposeful life.

Although Lara's home base changes often, the world is her playground and her home is within herself as she travels. She is most lit up near an ocean, hiking in the mountains, or having a simple meal with her family and friends. Mother to two amazing young men, Lara is welcoming in a new chapter of her growing family of daughters-in-law and grandchildren. She is a Butler University graduate, coaching certified, and a Reiki Master/Teacher.

In her #1 best-selling Amazon book, *More Than Enough: Discover Your Limitless Potential and Live Your Bravest Dream* (2015), Lara guides others through transition while reaching for their bravest dream. In her international best-selling books she co-authored, *Midlife Transformation: Redefining Life, Love, Health and Success* (2016), Lara tells her story entitled "God-Spark" and in, *Courageous Hearts* (2017), Lara describes her courageous path in "Finding My Happy."

For more information, visit, LaraJaye.com

References

1. https://getfitforbirth.com/a-mothers-emotions-affect-her-unborn-child/

2. https://www.developmentalscience.com/blog/2018/10/1/can-a-pregnant-womans-experience-influence-her-babys-temperament

3. https://news.northwestern.edu/stories/2022/09/mothers-stress-rollercoaster-while-pregnant-linked-to-negative-emotions-in-babies/

4. http://www.valueoptions.com/spotlight_YIW/pdfs/articles/Adult_Children_of_People_With_Alcoholism_Healing_the_Wounds.pdf

5. https://www.healthline.com/health/alcohol/adult-children-of-alcoholics#low-self-esteem, children of alcoholics

6. https://www.sciencefriday.com/articles/the-truth-about-imaginary-friends/

7. https://www.psychologytoday.com/us/bl

8. https://www.dailyom.com/inspiration/words-are-energy/

9. https://www.verywellmind.com/what-is-a-confirmation-bias-2795024

10. https://www.verywellmind.com/
what-is-a-confirmation-bias-2795024

11. https://www.amandalinettemeder.com/blog/2013/12/16/
what-is-a-spirit-portal

12 https://en.wikipedia.org/wiki/Ley_line

13. https://indie88.com/
what-is-a-spiritual-ley-lines-map-and-why-you-may-live-on-one/

14. https://www.areyouawakening.com/awakening-rants/
happening-now-timeline-jumping/

15. https://www.areyouawakening.com/awakening-rants/
happening-now-timeline-jumping/

www.ingramcontent.com/pod-product-compliance
Lightning Source LLC
Chambersburg PA
CBHW070542010526
44118CB00012B/1186